Beyond the Boundaries

Beyond the Boundaries
The Life & Times of
Dr. Jeff The Rocky Mountain Vet

Melinda Grohol

Willtreestraw Publishing
Mentor, Ohio

Cover photo: Chas Isenhart, 2024
Back cover photo: Spay USA Network Newsletter, Vol 3 No 3, 1995
Cover design and book layout: Melinda Grohol

ISBN 979-8-9986225-0-2

Willtreestraw Publishing
Mentor, Ohio
willtreestrawpublishing@outlook.com

~ Dedication ~

To Dr. Jeff, thank you for trusting me to tell your story

*To my daughter, Ginny, whose belief and support of me
and this book has helped make it a reality*

*To all animals,
may you always have access to a kind,
affordable veterinarian like Dr. Jeff
to help with your care and well-being*

Contents

FOREWORD
By Esther Mechler

Esther Mechler is the founder of two national spay/neuter programs, SPAY USA, and Feline Fix by Five Months, as well as the nonprofit United Spay Alliance. These organizations connect pet owners with a national network of veterinarians providing low-cost spay/neuter services.

My first image of him was of a long-haired man standing next to an old school bus. It was 1993. Turns out that old school bus was really a mobile spay clinic, and the man—an idealistic, ground-breaking young veterinarian named Jeff Young.

We met formally in August of 1993, when SPAY USA held its first national conference at Bentley College in Waltham, Massachusetts. Jeff was invited to be a presenter at the conference because he had come up with a unique way to bring spay/neuter services to people in need. At that time people didn't even know the word "spay" and often used the words "sprayed" or "spaded." We appreciated Jeff's creativity and finding a way to deliver services which were not even clear to most people at the time!

Jeff saw early on that much animal suffering could be prevented. If far fewer litters of dogs and cats were born, there would not be the extent of neglect and cruelty, homelessness, and hunger that so many of these animals suffer. The shelters would not be so overcrowded. There would be enough good, permanent homes for the cats and dogs that were born.

Jeff's earliest spay/neuter clinic, a school bus which he bought for $7,500 and outfitted for an additional $7,500, brought his services to the people in rural areas whose animals needed help. Taking the services to the people took away their excuses for not getting their animals spayed or neutered and helped him live his philosophy, "think globally, act locally."

During the next two decades after that first national conference, Jeff and I were invited to speak about the impact and importance of spay/neuter programs in places like Budapest and Istanbul, Hong Kong and Sydney,

1

Bratislava and Sofia. The interest was high, vibrant networks were formed and people saw how effective spay/neuter was; it was preventing animal suffering and overpopulation rather than trying to react to it at great cost and energy. The movement was, and continues to be, proactive and successful.

Over the ensuing years, Jeff became an important part of the ever-broadening movement to mainstream spay/neuter, to make it popular and affordable. Between 1990 and 2010, the animal shelter euthanasia numbers dropped 80%, from 12 million annually to three million.

Fast forward 30 years and that same man I met in 1993 is now the well-known and much-loved "Rocky Mountain Vet" whose television show was #1 for eight seasons on the Animal Planet network. This book is the inspiring story of a veterinarian who sees clearly, speaks frankly, works tirelessly, and has touched not only a multitude of human lives but has saved hundreds of thousands of animal lives—companion animals and wildlife alike—through spay/neuter, affordable care, and paying it forward. Helping animals and people all over the world—this is what Dr. Jeff does, what he loves. And this is his story.

Esther Mechler

Esther Mechler in Peru

*Jeff endorsing the Feline Fix
by Five Months program with
a banner displayed at the
Planned Pethood clinic*

PROLOGUE

Most of us go through life living within the boundaries of what has been prescribed for us. Sometimes we think about the bigger picture—what might be done to help or address the numerous concerns and causes that are presented to us daily via the media or personal ones that concern us. Most of the time, however, we participate sparingly or leave the larger causes to other folks.

What if there was an inspiring story about a real, everyday person who could take us beyond the boundaries to show us what's possible in the world of animal care and justice? A story that was also educational, illustrated, intriguing, informational, and shows what is possible when it comes to working with animals?

Believe it or not, this book project all started with channel surfing when I came across the Animal Planet television show, *Dr. Jeff Rocky Mountain Vet*. The subject of the show, Dr. Jeff Young, was not your usual looking vet in a white coat nor in a pastoral setting. In fact, he looked like a left-over hippie—a mountain man of sorts. After watching one episode, I was hooked. He was not like any other veterinarian I had ever seen or known. His top concern was helping the animals and reuniting them with their owners at an affordable price. And, by the way, he tries to save the animal first rather than consider euthanasia as an "economic" alternative.

Hmm, really? The animal's well-being considered above price? No patient turned away? Wow! That's a switch. How many of us have experienced rising vet costs and avoided taking our pets to the veterinarian or have had to put an animal down because we could not afford the needed care?

As I continued to watch the series, all eight seasons, I saw Dr. Jeff working on all types of animals, from exotics—lions, tigers, bears, wolves, camels, llamas, alligators, and more—to everyday pets. The exciting part, though, was that there was even more to his practice. From rescue efforts for dogs in puppy mills, to spay/neuter initiatives around the world to control animal overpopulation, to two international offices, and provid-

3

ing training for new veterinarians. Behind it all though—the practice, the outreach, and the teaching—there was his overall mission: to help as many animals as possible.

Amazing, I thought. One vet really does all this? He just steps up, assesses what needs to be done, and does it with care and compassion while providing a workable model of animal care and education that really makes a difference. This, I thought, is how animal care should be.

I really couldn't stop saying "wow" and wondered how one vet, and his team of course, managed to do everything featured on the show. Was this for real? I mean, it could have been staged because after all, it was "reality television."

So I did what any savvy and curious writer would do. I decided to get the backstory on Dr. Jeff and determine if all that was presented on the show was real and true-to-life. If it all *were* true, I simply *had* to write a book about it and share with others the story of this really cool veterinarian who made a difference in the lives of animals and humans alike.

In my mind, the world really needs to see and hear more exemplary and inspirational stories as such; stories that expand our world and take us beyond the boundaries of everyday thoughts and practices, especially where animals are concerned. My storytelling mission was underway.

The question was, would Dr. Jeff talk to me? The show portrayed him as being exceptionally busy, with more than 100,000 clients—one of the busiest vets in Colorado—and he was, after all, somewhat of a celebrity after eight seasons on Animal Planet. But I had to try, because I quite literally felt compelled to pursue his story.

I crafted a letter to Dr. Jeff, including my writing resume, proposing a book about his life along with a picture book to inspire young people to become a veterinarian. As I explained to him in my query, I have this passion for writing about people and things that make a difference in life. No "Kardashian" hype for me—just real people doing real things. I sent the proposal via snail mail and then I waited.

I was over the moon when Dr. Jeff himself called me some weeks later, agreed to my proposal, and after meeting me in person entrusted me with the exclusive to write his biography. After multiple visits to Colorado, and after many hours of interviews with Dr. Jeff, colleagues, staff, and others, I had the real backstory of Dr. Jeff, an animal doctor who indeed does it all.

During my research for this book, I also discovered that there is a greater import to Dr. Jeff's story as it relates to a much broader issue—that of animal justice.

"Animals are in trouble all over the world," states Martha C. Nussbaum's in the opening line of her 2022 book, *Justice for Animals, Our Collective Responsibility*.

Nussbaum, an American philosopher and Distinguished Service Professor of Law and Ethics at the University of Chicago, makes the case that animals suffer injustices and horrors at the hands of humans every day, whether through the cruelties of the factory meat industry, poaching and game hunting, neglect of companion animals, or habitat destruction. She advocates that it is our collective duty, as humans, to face and solve animal harm; to create a world in which human beings are truly friends of animals rather than exploiters or users. Further, she maintains that action towards this goal is not an option—it is an imperative.

Animal justice? Dr. Jeff not only talks about it, he lives it—every day for the past three decades and counting. His story illuminates a real-life, hands-on example that inspires and teaches others what it really means to care for animals and to have our best relationship with them, whether we are veterinarians, animal rescuers, animal activists, pet owners, or simply people who love animals.

Here then is the true story of Dr. Jeff, the Rocky Mountain Vet.

Melinda Grohol

A scenic view near Jeff and Petra's new mountain homestead

CHAPTER 1
A NEW VIEW FROM THE MOUNTAIN

Sold! One Mountain Site Property
Ideal for Veterinary Clinic
Plus Extra Mountain Home Site

Fall 2022. Dr. Jeff Young, an outside-the-box thinker, mover and shaker in the world of animal care, decided for the absolute last time to relocate his practice, Planned Pethood International (PPI). He had opened the first Planned Pethood clinic on Tennyson Street in Denver, Colorado, back in 1991, then moved the clinic to nearby Wheat Ridge in 2016.

Regrouping after COVID, he was searching for just the right location, hopefully in the mountains, to accommodate the practice he envisioned—an expanded, full-service veterinary clinic and hospital, an international training center with housing for new veterinarians, and a specialized adoption shelter. It was a tall order.

When the opportunity arose to purchase such a facility in Conifer, Colorado, about 30 minutes outside of Denver, Jeff did not hesitate. The decision became a fait accompli bolstered by two other factors.

First and foremost, the availability and purchase of a mountainside home for him and his wife, Dr. Petra Mickova, located only seven minutes away from the new clinic. No longer would he and Petra have to live above the clinic as they had done for so many years, but they would be close enough that in case of an after-hours emergency at PPI, they could be there in a matter of minutes.

Secondly, five miles west of the clinic site was the Intermountain Humane Society (IMHS), a fixture in the mountain community for decades, which could provide additional animal care and services as well as pet adoptions.

Once acquiring the two-story, 24,000 square foot facility, major renovations began in earnest. Prior to Jeff purchasing the building, it had once been a church and later a barbecue restaurant, so it would be a huge undertaking to convert the 12,000 square foot downstairs area into a veteri-

The Conifer, Colorado location

nary clinic, while upstairs would become housing for veterinarian students in training. It would take eight months for the renovation, but with characteristic verve and drive, Jeff forged ahead and slated the grand opening of the new location for May 7, 2023.

There was a lot on the line: promoting and moving to a new location in a relatively short time; a brand-new community in which to do business and develop clientele; maintaining and transitioning care for current patients; and a complete relocation during their busiest month.

Grand opening day, Sunday, May 7th, dawned clear, cool, and bright. Starting at 10 a.m. until 4 p.m., over 200 people and animals streamed through the doors to get a look at the new facility. There were people of all ages including clients, family and friends, staff, colleagues, media representatives, locals coming to meet the new vet in town, the curious, and a myriad of dogs and cats with their owners.

A large, nouveau art-type painting of a soulful dog gazed upon the visitors as they entered. Bright colored walls of orange, green, and teal gave

L to R: Carlos Borges and Dr. Tony Rios from PPI Mexico, and PPI vet tech, Jess Soto

light and warmth to the clinic setting. Jeff, tall and unassuming yet instantly recognizable, was dressed in his usual attire of jeans, a PPI T-shirt, and sandals.

With every tour group that came through, one could hear barks and meows, exclamations and ah-has, and see smiling faces as Jeff and his team provided vivid visualizations and descriptions of what was going to be where when everything was completed. One also heard numerous offers to volunteer at the clinic along with declarations of, "I want to bring my pet in to this clinic!" and "When can I make an appointment?"

Adding to the event was the news that PPI had acquired the Intermountain Humane Society just up the highway, abbreviating the name to simply Intermountain Humane (IMH).

The acquisition, a win for everyone involved, especially the animals, now connected PPI with IMH under one umbrella of operation. The benefits were many: additional space in which to house and rehab animals from the clinic, more opportunities for vet trainees to learn spay/neuter, and an expanded adoption center with more staff to help shelter animals find a forever home. Plus, with the combination of funding from PPI and donations to IMH, the facility would receive much needed renovations and repairs to make it an up-to-date, quality animal shelter.

Reflecting upon the grand opening event and the days ahead for the new clinic, Jeff commented, "I was pleased and surprised by everyone that came. It meant a lot to me and it will be good for PPI. There is still a lot of work to be done, but it will all work out."

Just as he has for the past three decades and counting, Dr. Jeff at the helm of PPI has elevated people, animals, and veterinary services to their highest level. Dr. Jeff is the difference. He shows the difference and he makes the difference in the world of animal care, and his formula is simple: quality veterinary care and services, including spay/neuter, at an affordable price; acces-

L to R: Dr. Petra, Dr. Jeff, their dog Fred, and Esther Mechler on grand opening day

sible care for all animals; community involvement and outreach programs; working to save animals rather than resort to euthanasia as an economic solution; and training and teaching new veterinarians to carry this mission forward.

Whereas no one person or system can address or solve all the challenges facing animal care, especially for companion animals, Dr. Jeff's work continues to serve as a valid and worthwhile foundation from which to operate and expand.

Dr. Jeff in his now-famous
chili pepper surgical cap

CHAPTER 2
THE EARLY YEARS

S ometimes we are fortunate enough to know from an early age what it is that we are supposed to do with our lives, and Jeffrey Young is one of those people. "I always knew I wanted to be a vet," Jeff affirmed.

At a young age, how exactly that would happen he couldn't know, but looking back at the various events that have occurred throughout his life, along with the myriad of people who have come into his life, fate appears to have set the stage and Jeff became a vet-in-the-making.

For Jeff, animals have always been a part of the fabric of his life. Since his early youth and to this day, he has been involved with animals on so many different levels: from playing with them, observing and raising them, to hunting and trapping them; to learning about and advocating for them; and now to helping, saving, and teaching others about them. Jeff's veterinary journey has taken him around the world and back again, beyond the boundaries of what he ever dreamed possible in terms of helping people and animals.

With an air of self-deprecation, Jeff is quick to comment that his life story is "not that interesting." To the contrary, the life and veterinary career of Jeff Young is one wild ride full of twists and turns, successes, pitfalls, bouts with cancer (yes, plural), and dozens of other challenges that would make most of us give up, dream less, or stay within known boundaries. But not Jeff. His motto is "never give up," and he never has. The ride of his life, his story, in its forward motion and in its wake, continues, and so does he.

Jeffrey Dale Young was born on April 14, 1956 in Frankfort, Indiana. Of the baby-boomer generation and as a midwesterner, Jeff's adolescent experiences and family life would instill in him the character traits of hard work, loyalty, and community service—traits that he acknowledges served him well and were meaningful.

Growing up in the 1960s, the time of flower children, hippies and the counter-cultural movement across America, also led to another characteristic that, though later developed and often accompanied by controversy, would become a trademark of Jeff's personality: questioning and challenging the status quo, especially when animals were involved.

Life for Jeff as a young boy was going along rather peaceably until his parents divorced when he was five years old. Gone were the comfortable and known family dynamics of childhood, replaced by a new set of variable family dynamics as each parent remarried.

After the divorce, Jeff and his siblings went to live with his mother and stepfather who was in the Air Force. Following his stepfather's tours of duty, Jeff became a "military brat" living on various military bases, both nationally and abroad. Looking back on those early childhood years, Jeff describes himself with an alliteration of "H" words —hellion, heathen, and hyperactive as hell, along with what would now be called Attention Deficit Disorder or ADD. "I was also a little crazy and not afraid of much," said Jeff.

"I remember the time I was about six years old," Jeff reminisced. "My dad and I were fishing in Wisconsin at a lake where there was also a dam structure. At the bottom of the dam was a large water hole. My father warned me not to jump in because it was dangerous. He said I could be pulled down into the current and drown. So what did I do? I jumped in, bobbed back up and said, 'See, I didn't drown!' When I got back up to the shore line, I was slapped right upside the head.

"Then there was the time I refused to sing the song *Jesus Loves Me* while in church," continued Jeff. "The song says 'I am weak,' but I am not weak, I thought. And I said that out loud. I wasn't about to sing anything that said I was weak! My mother wasn't too happy about that."

When Jeff was seven years old, his stepfather received a three-year assignment on the Island of Guam in the North Pacific. Here, Jeff had to repeat first grade because he failed the first time around; he simply could not sit still. "I was kinetic like crazy as a kid," smiled Jeff. "Always have been and still am."

The three-year stint in Guam was both emotionally challenging and stimulating for Jeff. The hardest part was not being able to return stateside to be with extended family with whom he was close. Coupled with that was the fact that both his mother and stepfather worked so he was alone

Jeff, on the right, with a friend, in Guam

most of the time. Jeff would later come to realize that the time in Guam was literally a glimpse into the future; a foreshadowing of the varied world cultures and experiences that he would later encounter as a veterinarian providing educational and teaching lectures around the world.

Most interesting for Jeff, though, was that Guam was filled with a plethora of animals, some of which he had never before seen. His curiosity was piqued, not to mention his sense of adventure. The military base in Guam, surrounded by extensive forest and jungle area, included common animals such as deer, feral pigs, boars, and chickens, along with exotics and less common animals like lizards, chameleons, geckos, bats, crabs, and carabao or water buffalo.

"There were animals all over the place in Guam," remembered Jeff. "Once we ran a wild boar into someone's garage and shut the door. We had wooden sticks and thought we would kill it with those sticks. I got in trouble for that. I was always being taken home by the MPs, the Military Police, for being where I shouldn't be and causing a disturbance. My mom and stepfather both worked, so I just ran around like a heathen."

Wildlife encounters aside, there was another group of animals, while not veterinarian related, that affected Jeff's life on an entirely different level, health wise, with a condition that would not present itself until many years later.

Guam, a tropical environment, is plagued by the group of invertebrate animals known as arthropods, or mosquitoes. To control and combat diseases carried by mosquitoes, the U.S. Department of Defense in Guam sprayed the pesticide DDT daily around the island. Used throughout the world from the 1940s through the mid-1970s, DDT was sprayed from the back of slow-moving trucks, leaving a thick whitish fog in its wake.

Oddly, this mosquito-killing fog was somehow quite mysterious and intriguing to kids of the times. Accounts from around the world tell of kids running or riding their bikes behind the sprayer truck that was driven by the "mosquito man." Following behind the truck, the kids were engulfed in the cloud of thick fog that turned their eyes beet red. Despite warnings to stay inside until the truck had passed and the fog settled, escapades behind the sprayer truck persisted.

The Smokey Joe *DDT Truck*

"When I was a kid in Guam," Jeff remembered, "my friends and I would run behind Smokey Joe, the sprayer truck that was spraying for mosquitoes. Guess what was being sprayed? DDT. The spray was so thick you couldn't see. We were just kids and we thought doing this activity was the bomb. I am not sure why we weren't supervised or why we ignored the fact that you were supposed to go inside, close your windows, and close everything up until Smokey Joe had passed."

And those first early escapades behind Smokey Joe were not the last for Jeff.

"Later, during the seventh and eighth grades, when we were on a military base in Florida, Smokey Joe was there, too. Luckily, I did not feel the need to run through the smoke quite as much as when I was younger. I truly believe that the only reason I developed cancer [later in life] is because I absorbed all that DDT."

While the use of DDT was discontinued in the United States in 1972 and most other parts of the world by the mid-1970s "due to adverse environmental effects to wildlife and potential human health risks," the damage had already taken place. And since that time, both U.S. and international studies have provided three significant findings about the effects of DDT. One, that animals exposed to DDT have been adversely affected with many tumors and diseases. Two, DDT causes long-lasting contamination of environmental resources that does not dissipate with time. And three, DDT exposure is a probable human carcinogen.

As it turns out then, Jeff may not be wrong concerning his cancer and inhaling inordinate amounts of DDT, because to date he has battled three bouts of cancer. The first, blood cancer in 2014, was cured. The second, B-cell lymphoma in 2016, was also successfully cured. For the third bout, once again B-cell lymphoma diagnosed in May 2023, Jeff is currently undergoing treatment. This disease and its many forms, while difficult, stressful, and often deadly, has not conquered Jeff. Instead, it continues to inspire a resiliency and tenacity in him that he infuses into his veterinary practice and life philosophy of never giving up.

After Guam, the family returned stateside and followed assignments to military bases in Indiana, Florida, and Montana that provided Jeff with opportunities to reconnect with other family members in those areas, including grandparents, uncles, aunts, and cousins. During several summers in the 1960s and early 1970s, Jeff would spend time at his grandparents' and uncles' farms in Indiana. While helping with the farm chores and caring for the animals, Jeff's hellion nature often prevailed as he interacted with the animals.

"I was still pretty much a heathen, even on the farm," said Jeff. "I would chase the piglets and the chickens around. The turkeys never liked me. Those tom turkeys were mean and I would get them mad at me and run them around. I used to ride the horses, too. I would bring in the cows from the pasture and put the suction machine on them for milking time. Those were great summers."

Within the family farm setting, Jeff saw that all the animals, even pet dogs that ran loose, were tended to and included as part of the family. It was, in his mind, the way things were supposed to be and there was a connection to the animals, a responsibility that the humans should care for them. "The animals I saw on our family farms were very well-cared for," said Jeff. "They all had clean and decent pens. It was a lot of fun being on the farm."

Whereas his time on the family farms involved animals that were well-treated and important to the family, there was one summer during which Jeff witnessed quite the opposite in terms of animal care and consideration. It happened at an egg factory.

"I remember I was in sixth grade and I collected eggs in one of those factory chicken places," said Jeff. "I hated chickens after that. They were

15

the dirtiest, nastiest things in the world. I didn't understand [at the time] that we made them that way. We [consumers] have half the information. All I know is I had lice on me every day and I had to wash them off. I was always itchy. And the chickens smelled. All their feathers were gone, and their feet would grow into the cages. I would think, this is nasty and horrible. So I would go through and get as many eggs as I could and get out of there as fast as I could.

"I did my job," continued Jeff, "but I never thought of it from the standpoint of, what are real chickens like and what do they do? I would think about the chickens on my uncles' farm and the chickens there were not like this. Most of them had feathers and the eggs tasted good. I did not get itchy when I was around his chickens. As a kid, you don't always put those pieces together."

It was the beginning of an awakening for Jeff, a conscious awareness of the inequities and disparities that existed regarding animal care and animal welfare. Why, he wondered, were the animals raised on his families' farms so well-treated while those same animals on the bigger 'production' farms were treated so inhumanely?

He experienced the same scenario when visiting larger pig farms with his uncles. "I think of my uncles' and my grandfathers' pigs on the family farm," commented Jeff. "There weren't a lot of pigs, but they all had names and we knew who they were. Then I think of these huge pig farms in Indiana where I could hardly go in without a respirator on because it was so nasty. Feral pigs in crates. You don't learn or hear about that. Most of the large pig farms I went into were places where they put pigs in cages and 'grow' them until they are big enough to butcher. As a kid, I wondered, how do you rationalize that this is right?"

Jeff saw that the animals on food production farms had no "natural" life. It was as if there was an invisible line of demarcation, like segregation or slavery in the human realm, that made it "acceptable" for such discrepancies to exist and that still exist today.

"Is there no concern for the animals in these settings? How is this right?" thought Jeff. Yet unable to process or address these incongruencies and questions, Jeff put the scenarios in the back of his mind.

What he didn't know at the time was that there was indeed an organization working on behalf of animals—the American Society for the Prevention of Cruelty to Animals (ASPCA). However, awareness and enforcement of their welfare policy was often another matter altogether. It would not be until 1975, when the Animal Rights Movement began to take hold in the United States, that animal welfare issues would come to the forefront of public awareness and changes began to take place, albeit slowly. Little did Jeff know that in the not-too-distant future, he himself would become part of this movement and it would profoundly affect his veterinary career.

> ### ASPCA
> The American Society for the Prevention of Cruelty to Animals was founded in 1866 by Henry Bergh. It was the first and only humane society in the western hemisphere at the time. Its founding principle: the belief that all animals are entitled to kind and respectful treatment and must be protected under law.

Along with the Animal Rights Movement in 1975, there was a groundbreaking, game-changing publication by philosopher Peter Singer entitled *Animal Liberation* that Jeff would later discover. This book, an intellectual eye-opener, forever changed the conversations and outlook about both the human perception and treatment of animals. It influenced, and still influences, countless animal activist efforts and policies for animal welfare.

> One of the intellectual founders of the modern animal rights movement was Peter Singer.
> In his 1975 book ANIMAL LIBERATION, Singer advocated that animals feel pain and suffer just as humans do. The challenge he presented: if we think the act of suffering is wrong, how can we allow the suffering of animals to go on?

Topping off the spectrum of animal involvement for Jeff in his early years was that with wildlife, specifically hunting and trapping. Those summers on the farm with his grandfathers and uncles were not just about husbandry and agriculture. They also held lessons in hunting and trapping wildlife and game, whether in the rolling terrain of the Midwest or the mountains of Montana when visiting extended family.

It was a different era then. Hunting and trapping were accepted and common practices—a part of growing up and coming of age for boys, particularly in rural areas. It wasn't something one questioned; it was just done and served to "prove" one's manhood.

Interestingly, although hunting and trapping involved the aggressive action of killing animals, there were two "ethical" codes to be followed. The first was good sportsmanship, accomplished and exemplified by a one-shot kill and not leaving a wounded animal to suffer and die on its own. The second was responsible field behavior, where the hunter ensures that meat harvested from the kill does not go to waste.

"My stepfather grew up during the depression," said Jeff. "He was given a bullet and a gun and told to go out and get his dinner. If you didn't get anything, you didn't eat. I remember my first gun was a single shot 22. I wanted a repeater, a semi-automatic. I was told that if you can't do it with one shot, you can't do it with ten, so, learn to do it with one. And I did. I shot my first deer, alone, when I was ten years old, with a single shot."

Regarding trapping, the parameters were a bit different and without

Jeff hunting in Wisconsin, 1978

regard for the pain or killing of the animal. Jeff was taught that trapping was done for three basic reasons: to trap problem animals such as those with rabies or those needing relocation for various reasons; for recreation and enjoyment of the great outdoors; and trapping as a source of income. The other part of this teaching was instilling the idea that trapped creatures do not feel any pain and "need" to be trapped.

"I wondered how that could be valid. The animal didn't feel any pain? These are sentient creatures," stated Jeff. "It didn't seem right. It didn't make any sense to me."

18

Here again was a whole series of conflicting thoughts about hunting, trapping, and animal treatment that Jeff still couldn't reconcile. As before, he suppressed the thoughts in the back of his mind. Meanwhile, Jeff kept moving forward, carrying on the hunting and trapping traditions as expected. He not only became a first-rate hunter and trapper, he also became a hunting guide to others.

"I used to take people to Montana on hunting trips as a guide," said Jeff, "and I would shoot the deer for them because they were such horrible shots and all they did was wound the animal. I would sit there and wait for them to shoot, knowing that I would have to shoot that deer at the same moment because I knew that I would be able to kill it with one shot and they could not. But I never felt good about it."

Jeff also remembered another hunting incident that greatly affected him. "I can think of only one deer where my gun site was off and I wounded it instead of it being a one-shot kill. It was bleating and making horrible noises. It was awful. I ran up and shot it at close range to finally kill it. If there is such a thing as ethical hunting, I feel like I always tried to do that."

It would not be until some years later, when he was a sophomore in veterinary school, that Jeff would abandon hunting and trapping, finally realizing the extent of pain caused to the animals. "It's not something I am necessarily proud of," commented Jeff, "but it was part of my life and I learned from it."

Incidentally, with all the time spent in the mountains, Jeff came to realize that the mountains and the outdoors felt like home and a place where he could be himself. He identified with being a mountain man, knowing how to survive in the wild, if needed, with his hunting and trapping skills, cooking the food he caught on an open campfire, roughing it, and relishing in the wilderness and nature.

It was in the mountains that Jeff also discovered his passion and capacity for long distance running over the challenging terrain and at various elevations. Mountain life seemed idyllic. Everything was there that he needed, but he wondered—could he make a living as a veterinarian in a mountain setting? What exactly would he do?

At this time, now in his late teens, Jeff had some decisions to make about his future and his chosen career path. He had seen such varied treatment of animals over the years, from well-cared for and loved pets and farm animals, to large, inhumane farms for food production, to hunting and trapping for sport or profit versus hunting for food. All of this served to highlight in his mind the disparities with which animals were treated. The overall question was, could he really make a difference in the lives of animals as a veterinarian?

In the end, Jeff's deciding factor towards pursuing a veterinary career had nothing to do with animal welfare, hunting and trapping, or a mountain life. It was in a moment of need. That heartbreaking moment came when his beloved dog was hit by a car and died in his arms, and there was literally nothing Jeff knew how to do to save him.

"You know," said Jeff, "when you hold a dying animal in your arms that you care about, you want to do something—anything—to help them, but you can't. You don't know how. I think that, more than anything, is what ultimately drove me to become a vet."

CHAPTER 3
TRANSITIONS - FROM THE KNOWING TO THE DOING

With his high school graduation behind him, Jeff was on his way from knowing he wanted to be a veterinarian to doing what it took to become one. He had at least eight years of school ahead of him; four years of undergraduate work with a focus on animal sciences followed by a four-year stint at a veterinary college. What might have taken him eight years took almost twice as long because life happened and several things got added to the mix.

Soon after graduation, Jeff married his high school girlfriend, Debbie Kotzian and had three daughters, Amber, Melody, and Jessica. Amid the responsibilities of family life and while living on campus in the marriage housing section, Jeff pursued his college education, worked multiple jobs, and enjoyed running and playing rugby. There was a lot on his plate, but with characteristic energy and brashness, Jeff tackled it all, invigorated and determined to experience all that life had to offer on the way to his goal of becoming a veterinarian.

Jeff's undergraduate education started at Purdue University in Fort Wayne, Indiana. A few years later, he completed his undergraduate work at Montana State University (MSU) in Bozeman, Montana, graduating with a bachelor's degree in Animal Sciences. While at MSU, Jeff took a host of non-related classes that extended his time there, including agronomy, anthropology, astrology, scuba diving, and rock climbing.

"Why are you taking all these unnecessary extra classes?" asked one of Jeff's MSU counselors.

"Because it's fun!" Jeff replied. It was all in keeping with Jeff's over-drive energy and his desire to live and learn.

With veterinarian college now on the horizon, Jeff applied to, and was accepted by, the veterinary school at Colorado State University (CSU) in Fort Collins, Colorado. That acceptance led Jeff and his family to leave Montana and move to Colorado. The backdrop of a city environment, Jeff's home for the foreseeable future, was not quite the life he had envisioned because he was, by his own description, a barbarian—a mountain man who loved hunting, fishing, and trapping.

"My goal," said Jeff when recalling this time, "was to get my DVM degree, go back to Montana, and become a mountain man fixing dogs and cats up in Bozeman. I always wanted to be in the mountains, but the city was where the money was, and the family."

A trek at veterinarian school is usually straightforward; students learn the prescribed lessons, follow the rules, pass the tests, and then earn a degree in veterinary medicine. Jeff's path at CSU, though, was anything but straight. Time and again throughout veterinary college, Jeff would find himself questioning and challenging the status quo regarding animal ethics and justice. He would try to make practical, common sense changes to improve research methodology or promote better animal treatment, only to be rebuffed for his efforts.

Unseen on the horizon was a court case, scandalous press articles, death threats, enemies, and animosities abound, each disparaging his reputation as he fought to do the right things for animals and define himself as a veterinarian. But all of this was yet to unfold, however. Now that he was at veterinary college, it was time to get on with the program and pursue his chosen profession.

During his freshman year at CSU, Jeff once again noticed the boundaries that dictated how animals were regarded and treated by humans in both education and governmental legislation. The established doctrines in both areas allocated animals as "property," something to be regulated, and each group of animals had a different set of regulations depending on what group they belonged to: companion, farm, wildlife, or exotics. These rules and laws brought to mind the unresolved discrepancies and injustices towards animals that Jeff had experienced in his youth. The question still in his mind was, "Where is the concern for the animal or is it only about how humans can benefit from using or having the animal?"

"My freshman year of vet school, 1985," remembered Jeff, "was the first year that vet students saw a film, not an actual experiment, of a rabbit being given a dose of penicillin, to which it had an allergic reaction, severe anaphylaxis, and it died. Before this film (CSU Veterinary College was founded in 1904), they literally did the actual experiment every year. They brought the rabbit in, injected it, watched it die, and then threw it away. Why? Why didn't they film it sooner? Why was it necessary to see this reaction, rather than just read about it, and then kill a perfectly healthy animal?"

During his sophomore year in vet school, Jeff took a 30-hour a week job at the Larimer County local humane society doing animal control. As he picked up stray animals, he noticed that pet overpopulation was a significant problem.

"At the time," recalled Jeff, "we were killing about 24 million shelter animals a year in the United States."

Not only was overpopulation and euthanasia a problem at the shelter, so was the abuse and neglect of healthy companion an-

> WHAT IS ANIMAL CONTROL?
> Animal Control, a local government organization, is intended to keep humans and animals safe. Services and ordinances vary widely with each locale and include picking up strays and problem animals; operating shelters and adoption programs for unwanted pets; disposing of animals; enforcing ordinances such as leash laws, vaccinations, and humane treatment; and cruelty investigations.

imals. Despite his discomfiture, but hoping to contribute new ideas for change, Jeff continued his work at the humane society, even being elected to its board of directors within the year. Notably, within a year thereafter, he would be booted from the board because of his "belligerent attitude and unwillingness to compromise" per the board's then executive director.

Meanwhile, in a neurology class at CSU, Jeff experienced what was for him a profound and startling cognizance concerning animals and pain. Throughout his youth, he had been indoctrinated with the thought that animals do not feel pain, hence the justification and absolution that it was acceptable to hunt and trap. The fact was, this teaching was erroneous; it had desensitized him to the pain experienced by animals, especially wildlife.

"I came to understand," acknowledged Jeff, "that animals do indeed feel pain. They have the same neuroreceptors, the same pain receptors that we [humans] have. Every person and every animal is different with pain and pain is a very real and individual response for both humans and animals. Animals are sentient beings."

This realization evoked a deep empathy for animals within Jeff's consciousness and he literally stopped hunting. Never again would he hunt or trap animals for sport, pleasure, or food—activities that he now understood caused great pain to animals, and activities that, in this modern day, were totally needless. And he would, in turn, become a vegetarian.

At the conclusion of his sophomore year, Jeff was awarded the Robert Rubin Memorial Award by the CSU College of Veterinary Medicine & Biomedical Sciences "in recognition of special attributes and promise for the future," or progressive thinking, so to speak. Ironically, this attribute of progressive thinking would, in the next series of months, be met with disdain and discontent by the very administration that originally gave Jeff the award for thinking outside of the box.

Jeff's propensity for upsetting and challenging the status quo regarding animal treatment and welfare escalated during his junior year with clinical and surgical experiences. During this time, as part of the required curriculum, Jeff participated in studies involving vivisection (operations on live animals), biomedical experiments and research, and other surgical experiences. He saw, firsthand, the violations regarding animal welfare and treatment. Animals were being used, mistreated, inflicted with pain, all in the name of science and learning. He began to speak out against the injustices, first taking his concerns to the school administration. When they didn't listen, he spoke to the local media.

The climax came during his senior year when he was asked by CSU to do research and a presentation on pound seizure, the results of which caused huge controversy both on the campus and citywide, involved a major court battle, and tarnished his reputation in the veterinary community and with his peers.

"I was asked to research pound seizure," Jeff recalled. "I discovered that CSU, my vet school, was participating with the local shelter in the practice of red tagging—where healthy, amiable dogs and cats were isolated, without the opportunity for adoption, to be sold to buyers of research animals. Then, these tagged animals were used in non-survival surgery where they were euthanized before recovering from anesthesia. Pound seizure, red-tagging, and non-survival surgery just promoted redundant research, like the rabbit experiment from my freshman year. All of it demonstrated a horrible treatment of animals."

> *POUND SEIZURE*
> is the sale or release of dogs and cats from a pound or shelter to a research, testing, or educational facility. Beginning in the 1940s, many states passed laws that required pounds and shelters to release dogs and cats to research laboratories. Today, while several states have banned pound seizure, other states allow it, and most states have no law either way leaving the matter to local jurisdiction.

Jeff continued, "I spoke out about my findings in front of my class and people were just like vipers. They were angry and hostile because they thought they would be deprived of animals on which they could get their surgical experience. Then, later, because of my research, I testified against pound seizure in court. I didn't know that one of my professors was testifying in support of pound seizure at the same time. My testimony won out and a bill against pound seizure was passed."

The backlash of antagonism that followed from Jeff's classmates, not to mention the CSU administration, was deeply critical and severe. Newspaper articles at the time recorded comments from CSU students and faculty that ranged from the dismissive to the derogatory.

One fellow student commented, "Jeff's attempts to do something different were off-base." Another student stated, "He's making a lot of people mad. He's kind of giving the school a backstabbing." Yet another remark, this one from a CSU professor, likened Jeff's brain to "a small brain shrunken in formaldehyde."

As a counter balance, Jeff's unwavering rebuttal appeared in those newspaper articles as well: "By pursuing animal rights," stated Jeff, "I raise the status of vets and I raise the status of pet owners. Who's in a better position than us [veterinarians] to enforce animal rights?"

Despite all the fur that flew, feathers ruffled, and apple carts upset, Jeff was never suspended or dismissed from CSU. He was, however, labeled as an extreme activist and a rabble rouser.

"After the bill was passed banning pound seizure," said Jeff, "a lot of my fellow students moaned, 'Now we're not going to have any animals to do surgery on.' So I gave them a ten-point plan to work with the humane society for surgeries that were needed to make animals more adoptable. I said, look, we have these animals in the shelters that need to be spayed or neutered or they need a broken leg fixed. We can do that, for all the shelters in the area, at a better price than buying the animals, and we'll get the practice we need."

The plan put forth by Jeff, progressive for its time and prior to the internet and other online resources, included the following highlights:

- Gaining surgical experience from cadaver surgery as opposed to vivisection (operations on live animals) as emulated by other major universities
- Computer simulations and videos of surgeries as reference material
- Vet student rotation through local shelters performing exams and surgeries as needed, including spay/neuter
- An indigent pet care program utilizing vet students
- Informational programs for the public, especially in schools, to educate them on the necessities of spaying and neutering their pets as a way to reduce pet overpopulation.

"Their reply," said Jeff, "was, 'Oh, no, we can't do something like that. It would cost more and require too much supervision.'

"Well, they do that now!" exclaimed Jeff. "But at the time, because I was pushing it, they wouldn't do it, especially because it was a huge scandal in the newspapers."

Shaking his head, Jeff continued, "I had a lot of enemies at that school. I had my life threatened several times, not that I was ever afraid, but people pushed back a lot. I never understood that because, from my standpoint, I just did the research and made a decision based on what I thought was common sense. They couldn't just say, well, we kind of get your point, or we disagree. They were vicious."

At the same time, there were students who *did* agree with Jeff's findings and proposals about animal treatment, but they were too afraid to speak up. Instead, they put notes in his locker about a lot of other unethical occurrences, expecting that Jeff would address the injustices.

"They figured," said Jeff, "that because I had already upset the apple cart I would continue to be the scapegoat. I was always going to the news-papers about one thing or another."

Jeff's plight of garnering enemies and causing upheaval with the edu-cational administration continued when he also protested the practices of the CSU veterinary hospital and their treatment of the Greyhound dogs sent over from the local dog track.

"They were bringing in Greyhounds from the tracks and using them for blood donors, to experiment on, and do different things," recounted Jeff. "My position was, why? We touted having some of the best care in the world for animals yet we bring these Greyhounds in and we don't take care of them; we don't treat them well. We use them. It made no sense to me."

Here again, Jeff was rocking the boat. In his heart and mind, he could not reconcile the hurt and pain inflicted on the animals in the name of research or experimentation. This exploitation of animals was simply not acceptable and he could not remain quiet.

"Yes, I often upset the status quo," said Jeff. "To this day, that is what I do best. If you have something that is status quo, right there you know that it's wrong because there is nothing that goes on forever and doesn't have to change, evolve, or get better."

All of this was further evidence supporting Jeff's drive for both animal justice and compassionate care. Soon after the Greyhound incident, Jeff started both the CSU Animal Rights Group and Veterinarians for Animal Rights at CSU.

"These groups don't exist anymore," commented Jeff, "but they were around for quite a few years after I left. The point is, I didn't plan on being a radical left or radical right where animals were concerned. I just tried to do some common sense stuff."

As if all these incidents were not enough, rounding out Jeff's sopho-more and junior years at CSU were two other significant events. The first, his failing marriage, led to a separation in his sophomore year followed by a divorce during his junior year. After the divorce, he became a single par-ent to his three girls.

The second event was marked by his meeting and friendship with Liz Gernard, an animal rights activist and vegan who worked at the same animal control facility as Jeff.

"She opened my eyes about a lot of stuff," said Jeff. "Liz was a hard-core animal activist and before long we were doing Fur-Free Fridays and Veal is Murder campaigns. This was the kind of stuff I fell into. My involvement wasn't necessarily because I believed in everything wholeheartedly, but there was merit to what was being done and at least I wasn't getting death threats or backlash."

Jeff was beginning to learn, though, that there was a big difference between being an animal *rights* activist versus an animal *welfare* activist and how these two labels related to yet another label of being an *animal activist* in general.

Simply stated, keeping in mind that there are extremes and exceptions within each philosophy, animal rights versus animal welfare views can be summarized as follows:

The animal *rights* philosophy is based on the premise that animals are not ours to use in any manner whatsoever; not for food, clothing, entertainment, or experimentation.

The animal *welfare* philosophy allows for the use of animals for food, clothing, entertainment, or experimentation, provided that humane guidelines are followed.

Animal activists embody what might be considered an umbrella con-

> ### FUR-FREE FRIDAYS
> Fur-Free Fridays started in 1985 when two activist groups coordinated the first protest demonstration against the sale of animal furs at Macy's Department store in both New York City, New York, and Sacramento, California on the Friday after Thanksgiving.
> Its goal was to denounce and stop the cruelty, done in the name of fashion, to fur-bearing animals, and to campaign for animal rights and protection; to makes a difference in a cruel industry.
> Fur-Free Friday went global in 2008 and is now celebrated worldwide.

> ### VEAL IS MURDER
> Animal rights controversy based on inhumane animal treatment.
> Veal comes from male baby calves who are either slaughtered within hours of their birth or sent to veal crates that allow just enough space for the calf to stand. This confinement prevents calves from engaging in any physical activity that would develop their muscles and thus make for less tender meat.
> Calves sent to veal pens are slaughtered at 16-18 weeks of age.

cept encompassing both animal rights and animal welfare.

Animal activist philosophy maintains that every individual, whether human or animal, makes a difference and has a role to play in this world. Animal activists, whether advocating for wildlife, animals exploited for lab experimentation, companion animals, or animals raised for food, share a common vision: a world without animal abuse.

"Isn't that what we all are in the end, animal activists?" mused Jeff.

During his junior year at CSU, Jeff met another major player in the animal rights arena, Robin Duxbury of the Rocky Mountain Humane Society.

"Robin knew all the big-name people and groups in the animal rights field," said Jeff. "I met the founders of PETA, Ingrid Newkirk and Alex Pacheco. I consider Alex a friend. He has stayed at my house and I've also done lectures with him."

PETA, People for the Ethical Treatment of Animals, founded in 1980, is an American Animal Rights non-profit organization with nine million members globally. PETA opposes both speciesism, the philosophy that one species is superior to another, and the abuse of animals in any way, including using them for food, clothing, entertainment, or research.

During this time, Jeff also met several other movers and shakers in the animal rights movement, people whose work both influenced and inspired him.

Animal Activists

Peter Singer maintained that the interests of all beings capable of suffering were worthy of equal consideration and that animal rights should be based on their capacity to feel pain rather than intelligence. Humans have and continue to exploit animals. This philosophy forever changed how we regard and treat animals.

Jim Mason proposed that with the use of animals for war and farming, the agrarian society broke the ancient bonds and sense of kinship that we are meant to have with animals. Mason supported the growing role of companion animals as a way to reconnect with nature and rebuild the human/animal connection that has been lost.

Cleveland Amory founded the Fund for Animals, an ongoing organization committed to fighting the exploitation of wildlife and abuse of domestic animals. His statement: "If more people thought about what it would be like to be in an animal's place, there might be more compassion in the world."

These people included Peter Singer as well as Jim Mason—a prominent author of books on animal factories and farming of particular interest to Jeff considering his childhood experiences at the chicken factory and pig farms; and, Cleveland Armory who is considered the founding father of the modern animal protection movement. As Jeff became acquainted with all these leaders and their platforms, he realized the underlying motivation for each was the same: the integrity with which animals were treated and regarded, and the importance of the animal/human relationship.

> ### DOLPHIN-FREE TUNA
> *The movement began with a 1986 boycott of tuna organized by the International Marine Mammal Project sponsored by the Earth Island Institute in Berkeley, California.*
> *It protested the use of purse seine netting practices that capture and trap everything it surrounds, including protected species. Further, it promoted the adoption of dolphin safe fishing practices to prevent the drowning of dolphins in tuna nets, thus preventing dolphin meat in canned tuna products.*

> ### SAVE THE WHALES
> *On April 27, 1975, Greenpeace USA, launched the world's first anti-whaling campaign in Vancouver, Canada.*
> *This campaign sparked a global Save the Whales movement that helped procure an international ban on commercial whaling.*

"Soon after becoming involved with Robin," remembered Jeff, "she asked me to do more work with her and the humane society. It was one of those roads that I continued down. In addition to Fur-Free Fridays, there were the Dolphin-Free Tuna, and Save the Whales campaigns. It was all right along the lines of PETA in many ways."

Jeff's involvement with Duxbury and the humane society also led to his participation in numerous intellectual and theoretical debates held among the animal rights leaders. Aware that Jeff had grown up hunting and trapping, they would ask for his viewpoint on this matter and others.

"There would be these debates," said Jeff, "and they would ask me to be on the teams about different things like animal cruelty, and hunting and trapping. It was kind of ugly to get up there and admit some of the things I'd done with hunting and trapping," Jeff admitted.

His involvement with the animal rights organizations during his junior and senior years at CSU, although educational and purposeful, was not always fulfilling but rather unsettling. "I often felt as if I was being pushed to be something other than what I was so that I could fit in. It was uncomfortable and frustrating at times," said Jeff.

Jeff continued, "I remember an animal rights meeting in Boulder, Colorado. A bunch of my vegan friends were there and they saw me put honey in my coffee. They gave me a big lecture about what a bad person I was for using honey and how much the bees suffered. I walked out and never went back to that group."

By the time Jeff finished vet school, he had the reputation of being an adversarial animal rights activist; someone to be wary of hiring because he would not conform to given standards and served to work against established protocols for animal care and treatment. Hoping to counteract that image and start fresh, Jeff sought a position out of state and was hired by a humane society in Florida. Unbeknownst to Jeff, his reputation preceded him.

"When I got to Florida," recalled Jeff, "I found out that the head of the Colorado Veterinary Medical Association had already called the Florida Veterinary Medical Association who in turn had called my new boss at the humane society to warn her against hiring me. Despite their warnings, however, she did hire me."

Ironically, the job in Florida lasted only a few months. This short-lived job and his abrupt departure, though, had nothing to do with the fact that Jeff didn't follow protocol or procedure as required. Instead, it was the logistics behind the protocol that, once again, totally went against the grain of his core beliefs about how animals should be treated; logistics that finally pushed the line of Jeff's tolerance and determined the platform on which he would base his entire veterinary career.

"I remember the day that the shelter was getting in a huge number of animals for which there was no room," said Jeff.

"In order to make room, I had to euthanize 56 healthy puppies that day. We were constantly euthanizing at the shelter. The day I killed all those puppies, I decided that I didn't want to do this; that I was *not* going to keep doing this. I quit that job and walked away. My thought was, 'I am going to do spay/neuter. If I spay/neuter everything, I won't have to kill.'"

With this event, Jeff identified an overarching problem for animals that he could address and pursue wholeheartedly: reducing pet overpopulation.

This turning point became, and still is, the primary mission of his veterinary practice.

> **WHAT IS SPAY/NEUTER AND WHY IS IT IMPORTANT?**
> *Spay/neuter is the surgical sterilization of an animal so that it cannot reproduce. Spaying, for females, and neutering for males, prevents unwanted litters, helps protect against serious health problems, and reduces many of the behavioral problems associated with the mating instinct.*

After leaving the job in Florida, Jeff returned to Colorado with his children so they could be near their mother, his now ex-wife, and their friends.

"I was not yet licensed in Colorado," recalled Jeff, "because I didn't think I was going to be living there. I returned to Colorado in the fall of 1989 and had to wait until spring of the following year to take the board exam for veterinarians as that was the next time it was offered. In the meantime, I ended up taking a job at a convenience store. I lived in a friend's house, for $100 a month rent, and I slept on the floor. I worked out all the time and ran. I came home at night and rowed on a rowing machine. I rowed out a lot of frustration on that rowing machine. I was a single parent of three girls and I wasn't sure how my veterinary career was going to go."

In the spring of 1990, Jeff passed the veterinarian board test for Colorado. Things were looking up and he was eager to get started. Jeff recalled his first surgery, a spay, that, although not grand or easy, marked the beginning of his veterinary career.

"I started being a vet by doing spay/neuter work out of the basement of my friend's house," recalled Jeff. "The first animal I did was a big fat Lab in heat. Dumbest thing I ever did. I was sweating bullets. The dog kept bleeding despite everything I did. I tied off the bleeders, double tied, triple tied, and it still kept bleeding. I called an associate, Dr. Mark Chamberlin (a friend from vet school who would later become Jeff's partner), for help. Mark asked if all the major bleeders were tied off.

"'Yeah,' I said to Mark. 'I triple tied them. I am pretty sure that dog weighed more after I got done spaying her than it did before with all those tie-offs.'

"Chamberlin said, 'Close her up and it will be fine.' I did that and then I took the dog out to the backyard and set her in the sun. Sure enough, after about two hours, she was fine and walking around. That was kind of the start of my veterinary career."

Chapter 4
Takin' It To The Streets - Part 1

O ver the next three plus decades, Jeff's veterinary career developed through a series of concurrent events and he found himself "takin' it to the streets" in more ways than one. His overriding mission, to help as many animals as possible, would take him on countless adventures and lead him to practice veterinary medicine in ways that were beyond the boundaries both geographically and in methodology.

Just After Vet School

Along with his first spay/neuter work right after vet school, Jeff soon expanded his veterinary repertoire by working at dog vaccine clinics throughout the greater Denver area in conjunction with Robin Duxbury and the Rocky Mountain Humane Society (RMHS).

CANINE PARVOVIRUS INFECTION, PARVO, first appeared in dogs in 1978. Its severity and rapid spread throughout the canine population led to a multi-agent vaccine to prevent parvo and other virus-related diseases affecting canines.
Still today, the best prevention for parvo, highly contagious to both humans and dogs, and frequently deadly for the animal, is the DA2PPv vaccination given to dogs starting at two months of age.

"At these clinics," recalled Jeff, "we offered the DA2PPv vaccine which stands for distemper virus, canine adenovirus type 1 & 2, parvo, and parainfluenza virus. This vaccine and others were just coming into widespread use and now the DA2PPv is one of the core vaccines recommended for all dogs. The lines of people wanting vaccines for their dogs would often go on for hours. We might be scheduled to do four hours, but we ended up being there for six hours. It was very successful. We were offering low-cost vaccines and helping animals. I thought this was the greatest thing."

Have Bus Will Travel

Meanwhile, Jeff came up with the idea of developing his veterinary practice via a mobile clinic. Jeff reasoned that a mobile clinic would be a good way to start because it was less expensive than an office building, there was minimal overhead, and he could travel to areas that needed spay/neuter services the most. He named his practice Planned Pethood Plus (PPP) referencing both the spay/neuter platform, Planned Pethood, and the "plus" services that might be added as the practice grew.

Almost as soon as the idea formulated, Jeff found an old school bus that had been converted to a recreational vehicle that provided the basic amenities he needed—running water, a heater, and hookups for a 110-volt electrical system.

JEFF YOUNG AND HIS MOBILE VAN

After purchasing the bus, Jeff remodeled the interior yet again to add the necessary clinical equipment, including an exam/surgical table, cage carriers, anesthesia machine, sterilization unit, supplies, and extra lights. Total cost at the time for the purchase and remodel was approximately $15,000.

"I was later written up as being the 'father of modern-day spay/neuter,'" said Jeff. "I traveled all over Colorado doing spay/neuter in that bus. I was one of the first in the country to run a mobile spay/neuter clinic. People reached out to me all the time about how to do the numbers and different things related to a mobile spay/neuter practice."

PPP on wheels served three main purposes: 1) it took away the excuse that people had no transportation or access to a clinic that did low-cost spay/neuter and vaccines because the clinic came to them; 2) Jeff could easily travel to any area troubled by animal overpopulation, especially rural or remote places that had no access to vet care for their animals, circling back as needed to treat animals missed on previous rounds; and, 3) it offered the opportunity for public education outreach forums about spay/neuter and vaccines alongside low-cost services.

Jeff adopted the motto "think globally, act locally" to promote the understanding that we are all interconnected, that solving problems such as pet overpopulation begins locally, and each local action builds upon the other until it expands globally.

It can be noted that mobile clinics, albeit *not* for small animals as Jeff was doing, was an accepted and successful practice in the western United States during the 1990s. There were many such mobile veterinarian services for *large* animals with vets bringing their equipment to the animal since it was difficult to bring larger animals into a regular clinic setting. There was, in fact, an entire page of mobile veterinarians listed in the Denver Yellow Pages phone directory during that decade.

Incongruously, there were groups in some states that attempted to limit low-cost and mobile spay/neuter clinics for small animals, sometimes limiting Jeff's service area, by stating two objections. The first objection was that mobile vets would not be around for follow-up care, and the second was that mobile surgery conditions were not sanitary.

In rebuttal, two points came forward. It was noted that mobile vets, like regular vets, were reachable by phone. Also, mobile veterinary settings followed the same protocol as regular clinic settings, including sterilized surgery packs, use of sterile drapes and disposable gloves, and a surgery area that was always cleaned and prepped per industry standards.

Notably, in those states where restraining action against mobile spay/neuter clinics was enacted, the laws were challenged and ultimately revoked. The reasoning stood that since it was legal to use mobile vets for large animals, it followed that the veterinary profession could *not* set different standards for smaller animals. Thus, previous limitations and boundaries were removed and mobile clinics such as Jeff's continued and flourished.

As it happened, though, Jeff's work and his reputation, like in vet school, still came under fire—this time from local veterinarians, his colleagues.

"When I started doing mobile spay/neuter work," said Jeff, "the push-back from local vets was that I was taking business away from them. I remember doing a clinic in a small southern Colorado town. I had only been there two days. My staff and I were working like crazy. Dogs needing to be spayed or neutered just kept coming and coming. Then a local vet came in and started complaining, talking down to me and my staff about how we did things and why. This was the first time I realized how much I ticked off other vets. I was previously oblivious to that."

Jeff continued, "So I got to thinking. I had just done a spay on a 13-year-old female dog that had litters every year of her life. That local vet had 13 years to get this dog spayed and he didn't do it, but I did. Were all those litters really wanted or needed? What became of all those puppies? Why did that dog, especially in her later years as a senior dog, have to go through having puppies? I did not understand the indignation and criticism from that vet when I simply did something to help that dog—something that should have been done a long time ago."

While local veterinarians were affronted by Jeff's work, there was strong support from the community as evidenced by one letter to the editor of the *Pueblo Chieftain* newspaper. In the editorial titled, "Need Is Great For Low-Cost Pet Clinics," a representative for Fur Purries Cat Shelter in Pueblo, Colorado commented:

"We recently have been hosting low-cost spay/neuter and vaccine clinics offered by PPP which seems to be upsetting some of the local veterinarians. The overpopulation of animals in Pueblo is staggering and we're trying to help control the problem. Some local vets say that the care at these clinics does not match theirs. These vets have never visited one of these clinics. These clinics are not an assembly-line operation. Pet owners are encouraged to ask questions.

"If Dr. Young sees health problems, they are referred to local vets or, if possible, treated. Dr. Young has even made house calls to give shots to dogs and cats unable to be brought in for various reasons. His number one goal in practicing veterinary medicine is the care of animals, not the making of money. This is a concept that tends to be forgotten by many of our local veterinarians."

The Bus Tour

During the early 1990s, Jeff's bus tour took him throughout Colorado and the western United States to areas often beset by animal overpopulation, including remote locations, rural towns, low-income areas, and Native American reservations.

"Word just got around," said Jeff. "I had gigs all around the state any time I wanted. It wasn't hard to find work."

Along the way, Jeff realized that there was a more efficient way to use the bus—to also haul supplies rather than just as a surgical site where he could only do one or two animals at a time. As he visited new areas then, he found sites where he could set up to do spay/neuter surgeries for a weekend.

"Finding a space to work while on the road is not a problem," stated Jeff. "All I need is electricity and running water; anywhere like a community center, town hall, gymnasium, fire station or space where I can work for a weekend. Then, by using my vehicle to haul supplies instead of as a clinic, I can spay/neuter hundreds of animals before I have to visit the city again to get more supplies."

The Spay/Neuter Initiative Agenda

While Jeff's practice was making headway in promoting spay/neuter to prevent pet overpopulation, elsewhere in the United States it was a different matter. The spay/neuter concept, while utilized in a handful of areas throughout the states, was not yet a predominant practice on a national level. The prevailing mindset was that animals either reproduced at the will of their owner or as nature intended, so why intervene? The underlying myth was that there would *always* be homes for new puppies or kittens either by giving them away or selling them. If not, then the animals could always be sent to a shelter; but, this line of thought missed the boat on two fundamental points.

First, there are multiple animals in both dog and cat litters. Depending on size and breed, cat litters have from one to nine kittens, and dog litters have from one to twelve puppies. Doing the math, this means that in three years, and as young as four months old, one unspayed female and one unneutered male can produce up to 512 dogs and 382 cats. That is a lot of animals needing homes.

Second, animal shelters—both traditional and no-kill—have limited capacity, and most do not address the root problem of overpopulation which is uncontrolled reproduction. With both types of shelters, when capacity is reached and there is no more room at the inn, so to speak, animals are either euthanized at traditional shelters, or turned away at no-kill shelters. Those animals turned away often end up in the street, still reproducing, resulting in more homeless animals.

From experience, Jeff knew that the single best way to reduce pet overpopulation is with spay/neuter. Not only does spay/neuter break the cycle of births and finding homes for animals, but it also produces healthier animals in five important ways: 1) it reduces territorial behavior such as spraying and marking; 2) significantly lessens roaming tendencies since the animals are not out looking for mating opportunities; 3) reduces aggression; 4) lowers the risk of cancer; and 5) increases animal life span by three to five years. This education about spay/neuter, along with being able to afford this service, was what people needed and the very service Jeff was providing through his clinic.

In the early 1990s, Jeff met Jean Atthowe, founder and past president of the Montana Spay/Neuter Task Force. Jean became one of the main people who influenced Jeff in his spay/neuter work and through whose organization he would, and still does, conduct spay/neuter clinics at Native American reservations in Montana.

Atthowe designed the Montana Spay/Neuter Task Force to help Montana communities solve their pet overpopulation problem with education, sterilization, and local volunteer involvement. Each task force spay/neuter event, then and now, educates people about alternative solutions to animal overpopulation other than the cycle of euthanasia that she considered a form of violence and animal abuse.

Atthowe maintained that living with animals that are being abused is not respecting life in general and that animal abuse as such is a major issue around the world. Regarding the importance of spay/neuter, Atthowe's motto was, "Why mop up the flood when you can turn off the spigot?"

Although Jean Atthowe passed in 2016, her legacy and the work of the Montana Spay/Neuter Task Force continues and has influenced many people and programs. In the newsletter *Animals 24-7*, writer/editor Merritt Clifton and his wife Beth, specialists in reporting about animals and habitat-related coverage since 1978, capsulized Atthowe's life with comments from many of her colleagues, including Jeff.

> JEAN ATTHOWE, 1931-2016
> Moving to Montana in the 1980s, Jean became involved in state improvement programs including politics, education, and natural resource management.
>
> She founded the Montana Spay/Neuter Task Force in 1993. In the first nine years of the task force, Jean led the way in the spay/neuter of 57,289 dogs and cats in Montana through educational, community-involved, free events.
>
> Her techniques and programs have since been emulated around the world.

"Jean was a friend, a teacher, and a wonderful and compassionate human being," Jeff commented. "She always saw the big picture and was all about spay/neuter, education, and empowering people to be part of the solution, especially on Native American reservations in Montana, but also as an unofficial advisor to spay/neuter projects as far away as Armenia."

In further reflection on his connection to Jean and her work, Jeff noted, "Without Jean, there would be no Dr. Jeff. She helped to mold and guide me from the very beginning of my vet work. She was an inspiration to anyone who knew her in the field of overpopulation of companion animals. She always understood my rough edges and that my 'hillbilly roots' were my strength to move forward with my work. She helped me to see the big picture and always ask myself, 'Am I doing what will most reduce suffering with what I have to work with?'"

The Brick-and-Mortar Connection

While traveling with the mobile clinic was working well and Jeff was championing the cause for spay/neuter, other animal care issues came up including general check-ups, minor surgeries, mass removals, broken bones, etc.—situations for which he didn't always have the equipment to handle and which required a stationary, more full-service clinic environ-ment. That opportunity presented itself when personnel from the Animal Assistance Foundation in Den-ver took notice of Jeff's spay/neuter work. As it happened, the foundation owned an older spay/neuter clinic on Tennyson Street in Denver that they wanted to sell to someone who was a good fit; someone who would contin-ue the clinic and its mission.

THE ANIMAL ASSISTANCE FOUNDATION was founded in 1975 by Louise Harrison to "take care of the animals in Colorado." Their hallmark commitment is to spay/neuter programs and working with the underserved areas in the state. Their mission is to improve adoptions, prevent animal cruelty, and seek ways to improve the lives of animals.

"The price was $5,000 down," Jeff said, "and the deal was that they would carry the remaining $60,000 at a two to three percent interest rate. It was too good of a deal to pass up, so I said yes."

Jeff added, "I had the bus at the time, so I didn't have a lot of money. I got out of the place I was renting and I ended up parking the bus in Mark Chamberlin's front yard. Mark was a colleague of mine from vet school, and he already had a couple years of veterinarian experience under his belt, and he became my partner in the practice. I lived out of the bus for a few months until I got the money for the down payment."

Even after Jeff purchased the clinic on Tennyson Street, he kept the bus and continued doing mobile work on weekends to help pay for the clinic's remodel. Several years later, he finally sold the bus and the new owner drove it to Louisiana to continue using it for mobile spay/neuter work.

Now with a formal brick-and-mortar building in a local neighborhood, with living quarters above the clinic, the new clinic, Planned Pethood Plus (PPP) started its ascent as a landmark veterinary hospital and Jeff settled into a routine that consistently led to a seven-day work week.

In keeping with his commitment to spay/neuter, from the onset PPP established its main policy that all incoming animals, if not already spayed or neutered, would be spayed or neutered while receiving services at the clinic. To date, this policy has not changed and only rarely has it been an

41

issue or caused an owner to take their pet elsewhere for veterinary services.

At the time PPP first opened, Wednesdays were dedicated solely to spay/neuter, barring any emergencies, and the weekends were filled with "Spay/Neuter-Thons" and "$5 Tomcat Clinics" throughout the Denver area, along with occasional bus trips to outer lying areas and Native American reservations to conduct spay/neuter clinics. Living above the clinic site, Jeff was also available to check on any hospitalized animals during the evening or remain on call for overnight emergencies. Hectic? Yes. Problematic? No, at least not for Jeff who readily admits to being a workaholic.

As for the other surgical experience, especially bone and soft-tissue surgeries for which he would later become well known, it all started quite by accident.

"Spay/neuter was pretty much all we did for a while," Jeff said. "Mark was interested in doing bone surgeries and so he started doing them. I wasn't overly interested at the time. Then one day Mark ran a pin through his hand while doing a bone surgery and I had to take over. I finished the surgery as Mark talked me through it. I realized it wasn't that difficult."

Jeff continued, "It's a matter of angles and lining things up and you kind of need to have a three-dimensional image in your head. Having worked with tools and in construction all my life helped me understand how things go together. We never took any formal classes. We just did it ourselves and figured it out as we went along. We had a pretty good success rate. I've always been a little gutsy and not afraid to try things."

Surgical experience for any vet, new ones in particular, comes with time. "You can learn how to do any surgery by reading," Jeff said. "Virtually any surgery you need to perform has been written about, and now with the internet you can actually watch these surgeries online. You just have to be willing to try, and that's something I stress to anyone I'm training, whether it involves basic surgery like spay/neuter or a more complex bone or soft tissue surgery."

Melody Obuobisa, one of Jeff's daughters, became the office manager at PPP, and she remembers the early days when her father was just beginning to do surgeries of various types and how she helped.

"When my dad started out," recounted Melody, "he taught himself many things because you don't get a lot of surgical experience in vet school. After reading the text book on the surgery he needed to perform, he would get gloved up and set the book nearby so he could have it on-hand to reference as needed."

Melody explained, "Since he was gloved up, he couldn't touch anything, but that's where I helped; I was near the book so that I could turn the pages as he needed. He would read something and then tell me to turn the page, then he'd tell me to flip back so that he could double check something. My dad read a lot, and he still reads a lot. It's all there in the text books."

On the topic of animal surgeries, Jeff reflected, "Vet school doesn't offer much in the way of surgical experience. Further surgical skill is sometimes gained via additional education, but more often it's just a matter of doing it and being willing to try. You may or may not have someone coaching you. The learning is in the doing."

Jeff added, "I remember getting into an argument with one of the residents in vet school who later became a very successful animal ophthalmologist. I told him that if an animal came in with cataracts and the owner really wanted me to take care of it, I'd give it a shot. But the resident said he didn't think that was ethical...that I didn't have the schooling for it.

"For the record, I have done this operation a couple of times on cats where I've removed scleral-fied lenses that were causing glaucoma. I read about how to do it and I successfully performed the operation."

Thinking about the new veterinarians in today's world, Jeff commented, "So many of them are timid and afraid of making a mistake. As a vet, you can either stay where you are and work minimally or branch out. If you're not a specialist and you're trying to do something weird, just inform the client.

"Think about the number of vets in small towns where there isn't a specialist or there may not be one within hundreds of miles. So what do you do when a surgical emergency comes up? Say 'I can't do it?' and let the animal suffer? Or worse, put the animal to sleep for something that's easily correctable? You have to be willing to work. I don't care how good you are, you're going to make mistakes, and if you worry about those mistakes your life is going to be continually stressful. You get good at what you do and then you branch out."

The Running Connection and Coaching

Still a model of hyperactivity and kinetic energy, Jeff also needed a physical outlet to stay in shape. No longer playing rugby, running became his daily activity of choice, an activity at which he was proficient and also provided a release for his energy.

"As soon as I bought the clinic on Tennyson Street," explained Jeff, "I went over to the neighborhood high school, North High, and became a running coach for the fledgling team. I wanted to do something to stay in shape, but I also figured that this was my neighborhood, my community in which I was working, and that I should give something back."

It was an auspicious start to the beginning of a 29-year stint that fostered a series of events and relationships that would both anchor Jeff to the city of Denver and round out his personal life in ways he never dreamed. As a running coach, Jeff became a friend and mentor to dozens of young people over the years, many of whom came to work or volunteer at Planned Pethood and who continue to help today at his current spay/neuter clinics and other events.

During Jeff's tenure, and under his tutelage, the North High running team began to excel. Time and again, individual runners and/ or the entire team entered the ranks of local, state, and even national championships. Still today, there are a handful of runners Jeff has coached who have advanced to ultra running and who retain notoriety on state and national levels.

A team of North High School runners at a Native American reservation spay/neuter clinic

One of those advanced runners with whom Jeff has an ongoing friendship is Joseph Manilafasha. "Joseph is one of the toughest people I know for all that he has endured," said Jeff. "He's still running and is very successful in life. He has also helped out at Planned Pethood in many ways over the years."

Joseph remarked, "I have known Jeff for over 18 years, since my freshman year at North, and he's become a great friend over the years. He's helped me get perspective and insight on life, but probably the biggest thing I've learned from him is about being of service to others...to give more than you take. Jeff has more of a big picture outlook on life that most people miss. As he always says, 'Do what you can where you are, and then do more when you can.'"

Today, even though Jeff no longer coaches, he still meets with a group of his former runners on the first Monday of every month to reconnect and catch up.

"Sometimes only a handful show up, maybe six or so," said Jeff. "Other months it will be 20. We all have our lives now, but it's the connection that counts."

One of the strongest and longest relationships Jeff has maintained from his coaching days at North High is his friendship with Hector Martinez who was just 14 years old when he met Jeff.

"Hector showed up when we were getting ready to do a track workout for cross-country," said Jeff. "I noticed he was watching all the girls, so I started talking to him and when I asked him what he wanted to do, Hector said he wanted to play football. Well, he couldn't have weighed more than 90 pounds dripping wet, so I said to him, 'Why don't you run? You'd be a better runner than football player. And besides, we have more girls.'"

Jeff laughed. "It's the girls that got him! That's why he joined the track team."

"After I stuck with it for a couple of weeks," said Hector, "Jeff bought me my first pair of running shoes." And from that point on, Hector and Jeff formed an incredible father-son type bond that over the years led to Hector working with Jeff in several capacities, as an assistant running coach at North High School, as a vet assistant at Planned Pethood, and later as Jeff's "right-hand man" at the clinic overseeing administrative duties, construction projects, and computer technology. Hector would also become a regu-

Jeff and Hector,
"Batman and Robin"

lar on the *Dr. Jeff Rocky Mountain Vet* television series where he would frequently accompany and assist Jeff with some of his most challenging veterinary cases. So close did Hector and Jeff become that they were often referred to as "Batman and Robin" or the "Dynamic Duo."

Hector, who now runs his own construction company, reflected upon his relationship with Jeff through the years and the impact that running had on both of their lives.

"I believe running saved Jeff's life," Hector said. "It serves as sort of a meditation, and it's also hyper-competitive. It requires a lot of self-motivation and there's a drive to be the best. Jeff is wired to do that. Running and coaching was a saving grace for him. Both of us were so fit we could run and talk at the same time, and we talked a lot about life on those runs."

Hector added, "To all of us on the team, Jeff was a father, a friend, always supportive and non-judgmental. He knew my story and where I came from. He supported my family and the other kids. He never said no if you needed help. He changed my life."

Hector continued, "When I first started working with Jeff, it was out of necessity. I stayed longer because I saw how I could help and make a difference."

It wasn't until Hector was involved in a car accident and needed neck surgery that he decided it was time to leave Planned Pethood, but his decision wasn't easy.

"Working for Jeff was intense—physically, emotionally, spiritually," said Hector. "And when I left it was like a breakup. I've had so many amazing experiences with Jeff. All those races and how it felt to be with the other runners...our passion and our drive. It's been a wild ride...and I wouldn't change anything."

The relationship between Hector and Jeff continues today, both personally and professionally. Hector is not only on the board of directors for Planned Pethood, but he continues to oversee numerous construction projects for Jeff, at the clinic as well as at his mountain home.

Spay/Neuter Goes National via SPAY USA

As 1990 dawned, the overpopulation of dogs and cats in the United States, while a known problem, was still not being addressed in any significant way, with millions of shelter animals euthanized annually. That is until the founding of SPAY USA in 1990 by Esther Mechler whose grassroots efforts would spark a national movement to reduce pet overpopulation via spay/neuter. Esther would become Jeff's second influencer, following Jean Atthowe. Of Esther's work, Jeff commented, "She has done more than anyone on the planet to help the cause of spay/neuter."

The idea for SPAY USA all started when Esther made a simple visit to an animal shelter in Bridgeport, Connecticut in 1990.

"I saw the most wonderful creatures in cages, all waiting to be chosen," recalled Esther. "I realized, though, that very few of them were getting homes; there were far more animals to be placed than there were good homes for them. Then I found out that thousands of animals were being put down every month, and that even if I adopted 20 cats, it would make no difference."

She continued, "At that moment, I realized that the only answer to the problem was to prevent unwanted litters. If only wanted litters were born, then the number of unwanted animals could be drastically cut. And the way to prevent unwanted litters is spay/neuter."

But Esther also realized that the cost of spaying and neutering pets was too high for many people.

"So I asked my own vet, Dr. Arnold Brown, if he would do spay/neuters at a deep discount for people that I referred to him," Esther said. "He said yes, and that was the start of SPAY USA. I also realized that the problem was just not in Bridgeport, but all over the country, so I acquired a toll-free line, 1-800-248-SPAY, and went to work in my basement.

"For several months I worked alone, calling veterinarians, shelters, and rescue groups in every state. I was seeking those who would offer low cost spay/neuter and to whom I could refer people in need of these services. There was a lot of information shared and exchanged."

Then it happened...the SPAY USA phone started ringing off the hook. The word was getting around that SPAY USA was *the* place to call for information on affordable spay/neuter.

"The peak came," recalled Esther, "when *Cat Fancy* magazine did a story about SPAY USA and included our phone number. That was when the phone never stopped ringing! It rang day and night and I knew it was now too big for just one person to manage."

SPAY USA soon caught the attention of the North Shore Animal League (NSAL), a national animal rescue organization located in Port Washington, New York.

"Fortunately," said Esther, "the president of the North Shore Animal League was interested in having SPAY USA as a part of its organization, and within a matter of weeks we had two phone counselors, a computer program with a comprehensive list of service providers, and a small office." Today, SPAY USA is still an integral part of NSAL.

At this point, in early 1993, SPAY USA was well under way and thriving. Esther came up with the idea of holding a national conference for low-cost spay/neuter, the first-ever of its kind, to help promote the cause, and she began looking for participants.

NORTH SHORE ANIMAL LEAGUE
Established in 1944, it is the world's largest no-kill animal rescue and adoption organization, with global programming and rescue partners focusing on the plight of homeless animals and the importance of spay/neuter to prevent pet overpopulation
Mission Statement:
Rescue. Nurture. Adopt. Educate.
Major tenants: the inherent worth of all companion animals, and the richness and complexity of the animal/human bond.

Around this time, Esther became aware of Jeff and Planned Pethood when she saw him in action at one of his mobile clinics and learned of the low-cost spay/neuter work he had been doing since 1990. Esther knew that

Jeff's expertise and success with his mobile clinic would be a welcome addition to the SPAY USA network and she promptly invited him to speak at an upcoming conference in August 1993.

The conference, Making It Happen! Networking to End Companion Animal Overpopulation, was held at Bentley College in Waltham, Massachusetts on August 6-7, 1993. Over 200 participants came from 37 different states.

This unique event, designed to provide practical hands-on methodology for developing or expanding local spay/neuter programs, covered all the bases. Speakers at the conference included those from a variety of backgrounds, including the areas of fundraising, marketing, grass roots media, veterinarians who offered low-cost spay/neuter services, progressive animal control people who promoted spay/neuter clinics to decrease shelter population, people who created successful public education programs, and people who initiated legislative efforts to curb the number of surplus cats and dogs.

Promotional and book cover artwork for the Making It Happen! *conference*

As one of the first in the country to run a successful mobile spay/neuter clinic offering low-cost services, Jeff spoke about the process of running a mobile clinic.

"Initially, a mobile clinic seems fairly basic," said Jeff. "Simply buy and equip a mobile unit and go out and spay/neuter animals. However, without an understanding of demographics, a pinpointing of problem areas, an educational and support staff, well-written and enforced animal regulations, and an established stationary facility location, a mobile spay/ neutering program will not achieve its intended purpose."

Jeff's presentation also mentioned two other directives that provided for a successful mobile clinic. One, the aid of an advance team, a "neutering" brigade as he termed it, to pre-canvas an area and sign people up for appointments, and two, the cooperation between local organizations, namely the government administration, animal control agencies, humane societies, and the veterinary profession.

When all was said and done, the Making It Happen! conference was a huge success on many levels. The participants who returned home were inspired and empowered by practical, real-life solutions towards reducing pet overpopulation via spay/neuter programs. In addition, the conference encompassed working plans and programs that could be taught, replicated, and passed on—methodologies and philosophies that became a catalyst for the cause of spay/neuter to animal welfare networks around the world.

"The conference energized everyone," Esther said. "For the first time, personal connections were being made uniting all our efforts and giving voice to the dream of solving the problem of animal overpopulation with prevention and specific methods rather than euthanasia."

This event—quite literally the start of the spay/neuter movement in the United States—superseded all expectations and quickly gained momentum on an international level.

For Jeff, in particular, already regarded as a spay/neuter guru by many, the success of the Making It Happen! conference heralded a new horizon for his practice—a tangent trajectory of "takin' it to the streets." This time...globally.

CHAPTER 5
TAKIN' IT TO THE STREETS - PART 2

The Local Connection Goes Global

The Making It Happen! conference of 1993, intent on presenting solutions to address and end companion animal overpopulation, did indeed "make it happen" for the cause of spay/neuter and networking to solve a worldwide problem. In fact, because of this conference and its constituents, the spay/neuter movement was propelled forward for the next two decades as word spread like quicksilver throughout animal welfare networks both nationally and abroad.

The two-fold message was clear: spay/neuter was a viable and humane approach to the problem and there were professionals with hands-on experience and successful programs to help others organize their efforts. It was a win/win scenario for both the animals and human caregivers.

During the next two decades after that first national conference, Jeff and Esther Mechler were invited to speak about the impact and importance of spay/neuter programs in places like Budapest, Istanbul, Hong Kong, Sydney, Bratislava, and Bulgaria. The interest was high, vibrant networks were formed, and people saw how effective spay/neuter was in preventing animal suffering and overpopulation rather than trying to react to it at great cost and energy. The movement was, and continues to be, proactive and successful.

Over the ensuing years, Jeff became an important part of the movement to mainstream spay/neuter and making it widespread and affordable. Notably, between 1990 and 2010, the animal shelter euthanasia numbers dropped 80%—from 12 million to three million annually.

"I received my first invitation to speak internationally at a Dogs Trust conference through the recommendation of Esther and the North Shore Animal League," recalled Jeff.

"Once I met these people, and after I gave the lecture, I had high ratings and good reviews so they kept inviting me back. I've spoken at several of their annual conferences over the years."

Jeff continued, "During my talk, I go over what it takes to be global in terms of a spay/neuter program and I offer up ideas on how to do things to make it work in the community. Some of the material is geared towards veterinarians, but most of it is geared towards humane groups in general."

> **DOGS TRUST - WORLDWIDE**
> *Their mission: Working towards the day when all dogs can enjoy a happy life, free from the threat of unnecessary destruction. Dogs Trust collaborates far and wide to benefit as many dogs as possible. Its work endeavors to change attitudes and behaviors and to introduce sustainable and humane population management practices.*

After that first speaking engagement with Dogs Trust, Jeff began to receive many more requests from other notable animal welfare organizations around the globe, including Blue Cross of India—an animal welfare charity based in Chennai, India—and the International Society for the Prevention of Cruelty to Animals, among others.

During the mid to late 1990s into the 2000s, and continuing today, Jeff and Esther, together and separately, have traveled to a variety of international locales. To date, Jeff has presented his spay/neuter program methodology, dubbed the Street Dog Program, in 47 countries.

"Jeff was always a citizen of the world where his work was concerned," acknowledged Esther. "His motto was, after all, 'think globally and act locally.' I think Jeff said yes to all these speaking invitations in that way that he is so open to new experiences, travel, and life. These conferences led him to many new colleagues with whom he has worked ever since. He has inspired many with his methods and passion for spay/neuter."

The spay/neuter experts at a dinner in Denver. L to R: Craig Neilson, founder of Spay Global; Dr. Jeff & Dr. Petra Mickova of Planned Pethood; Esther Mechler of SPAY USA; and Dr. Marvin Mackie, developer of the QuickSpay technique

"As a kid," recalled Jeff, "we traveled to many places, including Guam and Japan, and I think it just opened me up. On the Air Force bases where my stepfather was stationed, we met people who had traveled to many places and they would talk about their experiences. The idea of traveling always appealed to me. I got to do a little traveling when I was a kid and now that I'm a veterinarian I've traveled all over the world. Culture is a fascinating thing."

For Jeff, these international conferences were, and are, more than just lecturing. They are opportunities for networking and outreach and seeing a view beyond that of an auditorium setting.

"A lot of people just lecture at these conferences and go back home," commented Jeff. "I always schedule something else in, like meeting with local veterinarians, touring their facilities, and visiting the local community shelters."

This practice of connecting with the people to whom he was lecturing also helped Jeff to identify specific locations needing help with the problem of animal overpopulation; areas that would benefit from the Street Dog Program and Planned Pethood's global outreach.

The Street Dog Program, started after the Making It Happen! conference, is one of Jeff's ongoing passions. It embodies his unequivocal belief that a recurring spay/neuter regimen, coupled with public education and the training of veterinarians, is the solution to prevent animal overpopulation.

Time and again this program would prove successful in locales around the world. Interestingly, while this program is a regular part of Jeff's work, it remains generally unknown to the clientele of Planned Pethood.

That is, until years later, when the Street Dog Program would be featured on a special episode of the *Dr. Jeff Rocky Mountain Vet* show during which Jeff and a team from Planned Pethood traveled to Galati, Romania, a city plagued by the largest street dog population in Europe.

The choice of this city was an instinctive one for Jeff. Having heard of Galati's problem during one of his after-conference networking tours, he vowed to help and subsequently offered hands-on assistance through his street program. After some lengthy negotiations with the local Romanian government and city officials, Planned Pethood was finally given the green light to proceed with the Street Dog Program in Galati.

The year was 2017 when the Planned Pethood team and the television film crew arrived in Romania for the five-day event. Along with Jeff were two additional veterinarians, his wife, Dr. Petra Mickova, and Dr. Tony Rios from Planned Pethood Mexico. Also on the trip was Susan Rieger, Planned Pethood's adoption specialist, who would be working with local shelters on adoption programs and dog training methods.

Hosting Planned Pethood for this program was a huge initiative for the city of Galati and, as many times before, the program would have a profound impact on many people and their animals, not to mention helping to solve the burgeoning street dog population problem. While the entire city was positively affected by the Street Dog Program, there was one for whom it was particularly significant, a man named George.

To follow is George's story and that of the Street Dog Program that occurred in Galati, Romania. It is a rephrasing of the episode titled "A Far Away Home" from Season 4 of the *Dr. Jeff Rocky Mountain Vet* show.

A Street Dog Program Tale from Romania

George was a captain—their captain. Every day, like clockwork, a group of stray dogs from the neighborhood came to the captain's house for food and water, and the captain never let them down. They depended on each other; the dogs received sustenance and attention and the captain garnered companionship. As far as the captain was concerned, these street dogs were his dogs and he was helping them out. This was his calling.

One thing troubled the 82-year-old captain, however—the number of dogs in the pack kept increasing. It started with four dogs and now there were ten.

"How am I going to keep up with the cost of feeding all my dogs and stop them from reproducing?" the captain worried.

Not knowing what to do, nor having the money to do anything else, George dutifully continued feeding the dogs because, after all, they needed him.

Tuning into a television news broadcast one day, George unexpectedly received an answer to his dilemma.

"This special news report is being brought to you by the Foundation for Animal Welfare Shelter," stated the announcer.

"Today's story is about an American veterinarian, Dr. Jeff Young of Planned Pethood, and his team who are in Romania to help the city with its street dog population problem."

The announcer continued, "For the next five days, the city is offering a subsidized spay/neuter program during which *all* community dogs, strays or those owned, can be sterilized free of charge. This city-initiated program, in cooperation with Planned Pethood, will also provide training for veterinarians as well as assisting the local animal shelter with new methods for adopting out more dogs."

George watched with rapt attention as Jeff and his veterinarian team performed actual spay/neuter operations on television while surrounded by a half dozen reporters and several camera people. George was filled with hope as he listened to the comments from both Jeff and Petra.

"Until you offer low cost or subsidized spay/neuter," Jeff told the television reporter, "you're never going to stop the street dog problem. That's the key—stop the reproduction."

Petra agreed, telling the reporter, "The people need to know what they can do about street dogs and how they can do their part. This newscast will help them understand how they can help and participate in this special program and others in the future. If everyone participates, eventually there will be no more street dogs."

Moved by the fact that Jeff had traveled all the way from America to help the Romanian people, and by the program being offered, George called the information line and told them his story.

"These stray dogs I see on the street, I feel so sorry for them and it upsets me," lamented George. "I've not met many people who love street dogs. I first brought in four, then another one, and then they just multiplied. I don't want more than ten dogs anymore. I want my dogs sterilized."

"George obviously cares for these dogs," said Jeff. "He's on a very low, fixed income. He's the person you want to get to because it's absolutely implausible for him to come up with enough money to fix his animals unless you offer some kind of subsidized or free vet care."

So it was that Jeff, along with Dr. Tony, went to the captain's house to sterilize his crew of feral dogs. On the way, they picked up local veterinarian, Dr. Cornel, to assist with the trapping of the dogs and at whose clinic the spay/neutering would take place.

One by one, all of George's dogs were finally captured and spayed or neutered. George was happy and the dogs seemed content as well.

"Without Dr. Jeff's help," said George, his voice thick with emotion, "none of this would have happened. Here's living proof that there are still people who want to do good."

Mission accomplished, Jeff and Tony were about to leave when George asked them to wait a moment because he had a "surprise." George then ducked into his garage and emerged with two one-month-old puppies, one in each hand, and handed them to Jeff.

"Please take these puppies to the local shelter," requested George, "so they can find them a good home."

Pausing at the end of the five-day, work-packed jaunt in Romania, Jeff reflected and said, "I'm glad we got George's animals spayed and neutered. I feel really good that we've also done over 500 spay/neuters during this trip to Galati."

Finishing the thought, Jeff said, "At the same time, there is a lot more work that needs to be done. We brought Dr. Cornel into the process and helped the shelter with its adoption procedures. It's a ripple effect. You plant the seed and hope it grows. In the end, you have to 'spay' it forward; you have to leave something behind and then the next generation has to step up and take responsibility. Things do change and programs like this, with spay/neuter as the emphasis, make the difference."

***

The Decade of Ascent

During the 1990s, Jeff's veterinary career took center stage, continually moving him forward on his mission to help as many animals as possible. He lived above the practice on Tennyson Street in Denver, a clinic where he thought he'd be forever and often found himself working seven days a week. This was not a problem, however, because Jeff was doing what he loved—helping people and their animals, and he was tireless in his efforts.

Dr. Mark Chamberlin, Jeff's partner at the clinic, ultimately decided to pursue a solo veterinary career and eventually left the practice leaving Jeff to carry on as sole owner. The clinic continued growing by leaps and bounds, establishing itself as a full-service, high-volume, veterinary clinic offering affordable, quality service. The upshot was a continued increase in business as people came to Planned Pethood from miles away since they could afford the care.

The fact was, and still is, the cost of veterinary care was escalating to the point where many simply couldn't afford even the most basic services let alone anything critical that required testing, surgery, or hospitalization. Planned Pethood offered a sliding fee/price range scale and flexible payment plans which significantly increased the odds that a pet might survive when a pet owner had little money, and, it made euthanasia the very last consideration rather than the first.

The bottom line, then and now, is Planned Pethood's commitment to provide affordable care for all pets with pricing that ensures pet owners will not have to compromise on quality care due to financial constraints. It was in the wake of this growth and offering of affordable care that Jeff and Planned Pethood became synonymous with compassion for animals above profit.

"I didn't get into this profession to get rich," emphasized Jeff. "I wanted to make a living but I also got into the profession to make a difference. I feel like that's been lost in today's world."

So it was, amid a flourishing practice of compassion and affordable care and 12-hour days—with people, animals, and staff coming and going—that Jeff continued doing everything else. From traveling and lecturing around the world, conducting spay/neuter clinics at Native American reservations, as well as weekend mobile clinic trips to remote or rural areas and animal sanctuaries. Jeff also continued running and coaching the North High School running team.

During this time, Jeff met a vet tech named Janet Hattlestad whom he would later marry. The marriage ended in 2013 and they had no children.

Jeff's plate, as usual, was certainly full and even overflowing. Busier was always better as far as he was concerned. Not only was it befitting of his hyperactive personality, but it also helped him cope with his lifelong battle with depression.

"I've always struggled with severe depression," said Jeff. "It's organic for me but keeping busy and involved helps me work through it. The busier I am, I won't be bored, and the better I do. Give me free time and I will procrastinate. For me, idleness is the devil's work, and always having something on the agenda is the real key. And the other key is surrounding myself with people who I feel like I've made a difference in their lives because they've made a difference in mine. I want to make a difference somehow, somewhere."

Nowhere was this desire to make a difference more evident than in Jeff's veterinary life and promoting the platform of spay/neuter to stop the senseless killing of animals. Jeff's drive and outlook in this matter was something he calls "spaying it forward"—an extension of the paying it forward concept. Intuitively, Jeff knew that for spay/neuter to prevail, to be adopted and practiced by many, a legacy of care and protocols needed to be established. The vision of such a legacy developed in his mind included three components: new clinics dedicated to low-cost spay/neuter programming, veterinarian training, and public education.

The question was, could he, or would he, find the right people to carry on the spay/neuter legacy that he envisioned?

The First International Planned Pethood Clinic: Bratislava, Slovakia

In 1995, Jeff was a featured speaker at a veterinarian conference in

Bratislava, Slovakia and spoke on his spay/neuter techniques and developing a street dog program.

After the conference, as was his custom, Jeff met a local veterinarian, Dr. William Hudec, known as "Chuckie," who gave him a tour of the area and the local government animal shelter where he worked.

The Planned Pethood clinic in Bratislava, Slovakia

The connection between Jeff and Chuckie was instantaneous and mutual. Jeff, who possesses an uncanny ability to ascertain people and envision the future in a matter of moments, knew there was an opportunity for

Jeff, Dr. Hudec, and members of the Bratislava Clinic staff

a Planned Pethood clinic in Slovakia with Dr. Hudec. This was confirmed that very evening when Chuckie spoke of his desire to own his own veterinary practice.

"Chuckie told me that he always wanted to treat small animals and have a clinic," said Jeff. "At the time he was working at the government shelter and had a very small space. I said to Chuckie, 'Why don't we just build a clinic here?' I also asked him if he was interested in training people and he said yes. So I helped him build a clinic."

Such was the unheralded start of the first international Planned Pethood clinic. No contract, no fanfare, just a moral agreement between two colleagues, soon to be friends, whose goal was to make a difference in the world of spay/neuter and pet overpopulation.

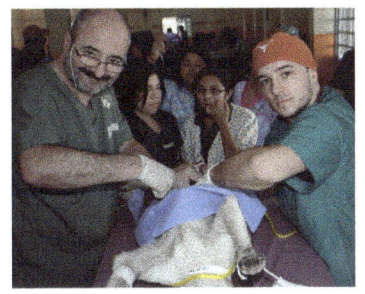

L to R: Dr. "Chuckie" Hudec and a vet technician at a spay/neuter clinic in Mexico

"What I do," explained Jeff, "is I pay for the clinics, I build them, I give people the equipment and say, 'Look, pay me back, interest free, when you have the money. Pay me back the amount of original investment and I will use that to do other spay/neuter work.' I just try to recycle the money as best I can."

Jeff continued, "Chuckie is like a brother to me. We just became really good friends. He speaks fluent Russian and has trained many Russian and Ukrainian vets. He came over here several times to do reservation work with me and I went back several times to Slovakia and other areas to do lectures and different things with him. We've done a lot of stuff together."

Hudec retired in 2022 and closed the Planned Pethood practice in

Bratislava. However, the Planned Pethood legacy and connections live on in Bratislava and the surrounding areas as veterinarian students from this region still travel regularly to Planned Pethood in the USA for veterinary training. Future plans for outreach in this region include a possible clinic in Montenegro.

The Second International Planned Pethood Clinic: Merida, Mexico

The second international clinic, several years in the making, began in 2000 in Merida, Mexico when Jeff, on Esther Mechler's recommendation, was speaking at the University of Yucatan to veterinary professionals and students on the subjects of early spay/neuter, before one year of age, and the benefits of the Planned Pethood Street Dog Program. These were important topics, considering that many areas of Mexico, especially Merida, were plagued by problems associated with ever-growing street dog populations.

Street dogs in Mexico

Tourists and visitors to Mexico, upon seeing packs of roaming, scraggly dogs were often frightened and deterred from staying any length of time. For the locals, the dogs were also a concern due to outbreaks of dog fighting, the rise in dog bites and dog attacks, and the spread of zoonotic diseases such as rabies, parvo, lyme, and cat scratch disease among others.

An even bigger problem was overcoming the prevalent "macho" Latin American attitude regarding spay/neuter in general, let alone *early* spay/neuter, that females were the issue, not the males. To further complicate matters, there was a belief that the spaying of females could not occur for at least a year, not until after the female had their first heat and first pregnancy. As for neutering the male dogs, that was simply not considered or permitted.

As with previous after-conference activities, Jeff again set out to network with local veterinarian and government personnel. This time, Jeff was paired with second year veterinarian student Tony Rios. During their tour of the town, its veterinary facilities and shelters, Jeff and Tony spoke of the growing need for controlling animal overpopulation in Mexico.

Tony, like Jeff, had a serious interest in spay/neuter. It was a fortuitous connection on every level, and as with Chuckie, Jeff felt a bond with Tony that would develop into a steadfast partnership and abiding friendship that continues to this day.

As was often the case with Jeff's worldwide travels, lecturing was not the only item on his agenda. The day after the lecture at the university, Jeff and his team were doing a government subsidized spay/neuter clinic in a city located two hours from Merida. This event marked the first such spay/neuter event in Mexico, and knowing of Tony's keen interest in spay/neuter, Jeff invited Tony to assist at this clinic and Tony agreed.

During the clinic event, Jeff quickly noticed Tony's dedication to the cause, along with his strong work ethic, so after that event, Jeff invited Tony to train at Planned Pethood in Denver. Jeff even went a step further and purchased a plane ticket for Tony's first visit to Denver a few months later.

"That was amazing to me!" said Tony. "I couldn't believe that someone who didn't really know me was taking such an interest in me. And the visits and the training didn't stop. I went to Denver at every opportunity until I graduated a few years later—every summer and every Easter vacation, which is two weeks in Mexico."

For Tony, there was quite a marked difference in learning styles between Mexico and the United States. "I remember clearly when I first arrived in Denver," elaborated Tony, "I was still in my second year as a vet student. I knew how to do surgery, but of course no one lets you. In Mexico, surgery was not a solo effort; it was always done with a team involving four to five people."

Tony continued, "Here in Colorado, though, it was different. Jeff said, 'Watch me for three days and then you will do it by yourself with my supervision.' What a difference! At Planned Pethood I trained with just one person on how to do everything."

By the time Tony graduated from veterinarian school a couple of years later, there was an undeniable bond of friendship and trust between him and Jeff; a father-son type relationship that would guide all their future interactions. As with Chuckie and the start of the first international clinic, Jeff knew there was an opportunity to make a difference, not only with Tony and his veterinarian training, but also with starting another international clinic in Mexico where there was a great need.

"Pretty much from the beginning," recalled Tony, "Jeff was clear about wanting to do a business in Mexico and a business with me because of my interest in spay/neuter and veterinary work."

Starting a new clinic in Mexico, while of interest to both Jeff and Tony, would present several obstacles and hurdles. This was, technically, an American coming to do a business in a foreign, male-dominated society. It would be a business that involved lower socioeconomic levels whose methodology of both spay/neuter ran contrary to long-held beliefs and practices. Both Tony and Jeff wondered if it could even be done.

There were other important factors to consider as well, concerning money flow and animal care.

"Money doesn't run in Mexico like in the United States," Tony told Jeff. "We do care about animals in Mexico, but we don't invest in our animals like in the states."

But Jeff was undeterred. He told Tony that he just wanted him and the people in Mexico to have a better life. He wanted to increase veterinary medicine there by working with local universities, authorities, and shelters to change the thinking about spay/neuter in this region.

For Jeff, failure was not an option; there could and would be a clinic in Mexico. Jeff's mindset was if he could build a clinic in Slovakia, why not Mexico?

"When I graduated in early 2006," recalled Tony, "I was 22 years old. I called Jeff and told him I was ready to start a business, but Jeff wasn't ready. So, while I waited for Jeff, I worked for six months as a helper to one of the teachers in the clinic at the university and I made $25 a month."

In the interim, Tony also worked at a small animal hospital. It was there that he learned how to run a veterinary hospital because to date he had only been a vet student. Later, as Planned Pethood Mexico evolved,

Tony would pursue additional business education to help him manage the practice as an administrator.

By the latter part of 2006, Jeff was ready to make it happen in Mexico and the search for a property began.

"We drove around and looked at different properties," said Jeff. "We found an old house. We actually bought it on credit which is really rare in Mexico. We went in and started remodeling. I helped and Hector came down and helped, too."

"Jeff has the amazing capacity to imagine and visualize future things," stated Tony, "As soon as he opened the door of the house, he pointed out the different areas saying, 'This is going to be the front desk. This is going to be the reception area. This is going to be appointment room number one, and number two. We can open a door here and go through to x-rays.' And that is what we did. 90% of what he described by taking one step inside the building is how it turned out to be."

Tony added, "And that's how Planned Pethood in Mexico got started. We got a really good deal in terms of payment. We were offered extended credit which typically doesn't happen in Mexico. We got one and a half years to pay with no interest."

While this was an excellent start, unbeknownst to either Tony or Jeff, another obstacle was on the horizon pertaining to city permits and operating a business in what was designated as a house. To date, all the transactions for the property had been conducted through lawyers and accountants and no one had mentioned this technicality.

"We were in the middle of the remodel," remembered Tony, "and my uncle asked me if we had the necessary license to have a business in the city. I didn't know we needed one so I went and filed all the necessary papers to put everything in order."

A month later, plans came to a halt when Tony received a property notice with the words NOT ACCEPTED stamped across the page. Extremely distressed by this news, Tony wondered how he could ever tell Jeff that the clinic in which he had just invested $80K was a no go. He despaired that there was no solution until he spoke with his uncle.

"My uncle, a notary, and who had good connections in the legislative areas, started looking into the law," remembered Tony. "He discovered this tiny provision that said because we were on the main avenue of the city, we were able to have a business in that area, even if it was in a family house as we were. Finding this law enabled us to get the license and permit we needed. I don't think I ever told Jeff about this part. But I suffered for almost six weeks until everything was settled."

With the house property now secured, the remodel was finally completed. Tony purchased startup equipment and made plans for the grand opening of Planned Pethood International Mexico (PPI Mexico).

"At that time," said Tony, "Jeff came to me and said, 'Well, this is your business now, Tony, and it's your turn to run it. I have no more money to invest.' Once in a while he used to send us sutures, but since the opening, he hasn't put any money into the business and we have been on our own financially."

Tony elaborated and noted, "Everyone believed that the American guy arrived with tons of money and set up the business and it was easy for me to build it. Partially this is true. But looking at the full story, it wasn't that easy developing a full-fledged veterinary clinic and training center. We started with just three people, two doctors and one technician. Now, after more than 16 years, we have a staff of 44 and run a full-service clinic."

The Planned Pethood Mexico staff in 2023. Tony is in the center of row two with both Jeff and Petra to the right

Today, in addition to being the lead veterinarian, Tony is also the general manager, CEO, and Public Relations person at PPI Mexico. Half of his time is spent as an administrator and the other half as a surgeon.

"In veterinarian school," explained Tony, "they don't teach you anything about the business of being a vet. I learned how to do all of the business stuff by having to solve problems and taking courses about business. Being an administrator, part of what I sacrifice is not being able to do surgery all the time. But I have people that do surgery even better than me. We train them and they are good at it. I have a really good crew."

Tony commented further, "Students come to us from all over to train here—Peru, Chile, different states in Mexico. One of the missions of our company is to share. So we share our knowledge and our techniques. We give them the opportunity like I had at Planned Pethood with Jeff when I

Tony & Jeff at dinner in Mexico

got started. It's all part of our duty and our mission."

Reflecting upon PPI Mexico and his role in the organization, Tony added, "I don't want to be a little Jeff; that's not my mission. But representing what Jeff and Planned Pethood represented to me is definitely part of my mission. I want to do it better because I totally believe that if the student doesn't get better than the teacher, there is no sense of life. Because the teachers are eventually going to die and then what? You're going to leave a generation behind the master. I don't think I'm even close to being better than Jeff, but I represent a lot of what he represents."

Tony, having long since repaid Jeff the original investment amount, now owns PPI Mexico outright.

"Jeff has always been my partner without signing anything," commented Tony. "We never had a formal contract. It was all moral honor and friendship. Although I am the sole owner of the business now, Jeff is still morally my partner and he will always be my boss."

"Today," said Jeff proudly, "Planned Pethood in Merida is

Children with their pets at a low-cost spay/neuter clinic in a small Mexican village

65

one of the busiest and best clinics in all of Mexico. They've expanded several times and it's where we have one of our International Training Centers. There's a room set up just for students and they work very closely with the University of Yucatan. It's not uncommon to have up to 20 students there at any given time. And, Tony goes out twice a month to small villages and does low-cost spay/neuter clinics; he helps the poor people. They're also teaching all the young kids about spay/neuter and community service work."

"If you ask me," said Tony, "after 23 years of knowing Jeff, and over 16 years at Planned Pethood, the main success is not the 30,000+ animals that we have fixed under Mexican conditions, it's the thinking that we've changed about companion animal welfare and knowledge about spay/neuter throughout Mexico."

He added, "Underlying the change in thinking is the component of education. A big chunk of this difference in attitude is because of the education program we have created by going out to the elementary schools."

A group of school children play a game designed by PPI Mexico to teach youth about spay/neuter and responsible pet ownership

Tony added, "We teach children about being a responsible pet owner and about spay/neuter. My wife, Silvia, oversees our education program, and I totally believe that's the future. I don't want to change local vets. I want to change the thinking and the mentality for the children."

Tony explained, "A big difference in our spay/neuter education program versus other successful groups working in that same area is letting the kids and the pet owners watch an actual spay/neuter surgery. When those kids come to school the next day, they talk about how they touched animal parts!

"I have pictures of my daughters, gowned and masked, who, with the help of a technician, helped sponge up some blood during a spay surgery. Having helped with the actual experience made their day. That's how we are going to make an impact!" exclaimed Tony.

The evidence of that change in the children then trickles out to their parents and changes their attitudes as well.

"We may not change the lives of those kids," said Tony, "but we really make a difference in their thinking and that of their parents. In fact, the parents sometimes come back to us and say, 'What are you teaching our children?! They tell me I need a leash for my dog and that I can't feed it chicken bones like we've always done!'"

Tony has also taught his own children well by instilling in their minds the importance and necessity of spay/neuter for pets. Knowledge about spay/neuter has become second nature for his daughters and they in turn pass it on with alacrity and passion to their friends and sometimes even complete strangers.

"Since they were born, my daughters have been in the spay/neuter world," commented Tony. "I have pictures of them scrubbing surgical instruments. Now, whenever they're in a social group and they hear someone say that they're going to breed their dog, they automatically say 'What?!' and tell them they shouldn't do that. Then they proceed to give their friends a clear explanation of why you should not breed your pet and that spay/neuter is more important."

Today, due to the efforts of Jeff, Planned Pethood, and Tony, the attitude about caring for companion animals in Mexico has shifted significantly and societal norms have changed.

"It's like having a cat or dog in Mexico today," explained Tony. "Ten or fifteen years ago, you knew that you should at least get it a rabies shot. Nothing else. Now you immediately think spay/neuter, and a rabies shot, and vaccinations, and deworming; it just comes with the package of getting a pet."

So it is, under the additional auspices of Planned Pethood Mexico, that the legacy of care and compassion for companion animals is carried on. Jeff regularly works with Tony throughout Mexico at low-cost or subsidized spay/neuter clinics. He also works with the students at the International Training Center in Mexico via lectures and training sessions.

"One of the greatest compliments I ever received," said Jeff, "was when I was told that, 'There is the Yucatan and Mexico *before* Dr. Jeff, and there is the Yucatan and Mexico *after* Dr. Jeff, and there is a *big* difference!' They even have a wing named after me in the training center at PPI Mexico."

Tony and Jeff with Marie Chenery and Dr. Terry Paik at a clinic in Puerto Morelos, Mexico, 2023

Another Global Connection

While the platform of spay/neuter to control animal overpopulation is being adopted around the world, there is always more work to be done in terms of outreach, teaching, and programming. Planned Pethood, a leader in this field, has been called upon many times for assistance. Another such opportunity occurred, and continues, with the organization of Spay Global, an extension of Spay Mexico, and the work of Craig Neilson.

Neilson, although not a veterinarian, is a strong advocate of spay/neuter and seriously intent in helping to advance the cause. He started Spay Mexico but then, following a decade of work, when he felt the cause was not advancing well, called upon the advisory board member, Esther Mechler, for help. Esther in turn gave him Jeff's name and number he contacted Jeff.

Craig went over the scenario with Jeff. "I've been down here in Mexico for over ten years," he told Jeff, "and the number of spay/neuters we've done via Spay Mexico is only a few thousand. We have the protocol for high volume in place and a good team, but I think we can do more. How can I further advance the cause?"

"We do that number in just a year," replied Jeff. "I'll show you how to do it. It's what I call the Montana Task Force Technique in honor of

Jean Atthowe. It's how we set up to do mobile spay/neuter clinics—high quality, high volume. We can do 500-600 animals in a day sometimes if we have the right people. It's not about being fast all the time; you have to work up to being quick. It's also about do-ing it right."

As Spay Mexico and Planned Pethood worked together, Jeff showed Craig the pro-cess to develop a viable high-volume spay/ neuter program through outreach, educa-tion, training, and collaboration; basically, the tenants of his own successful spay/neu-

> **SPAY GLOBAL**
> Its mission: to help end pet overpopulation through spay/neuter surgeries and training veterinarians in High Quality High Volume (HQHV) spay and neuter best practices

ter practice. With the successful growth of Spay Mexico came the idea of branching out and creating other spay programs worldwide.

"We started Spay Global around the pandemic in 2020," said Jeff. "I'm on the board. The idea we've worked out with Sonora University in north-western Mexico and several other area universities is a four-day online course followed by a hands-on experience during which the veterinary stu-dent performs spay/neuter surgery at a designated clinic event. When they successfully complete both parts of the program, they receive a certificate that shows they have the basics down and know what's expected of them when they do spay/neuter work in the future."

Spay Global has expended to include Spay Panama, Spay Argentina, and many other locales. "We have groups all over the place," noted Jeff, "and we are constantly sending people to lots of different places to further the program. It will take some time. We had to regroup after COVID."

Though the pandemic set them back a bit, the mission of Spay Global continues. Their five-year goal is to train 500 or more veterinarians in High Quality High Volume (HQHV) spay/neuter techniques and to have steril-ized over 150,000 dogs and cats, and then increasing that reach in future years.

Going forward, Spay Global continues to expand its programming, training, and clinic events. One such clinic was held in Sonora, Mexico in 2024. This training event, the first of its kind in the area, was a collabora-tion between two universities, the Universidad de Sonora and the Universidad del Valle de Mexico, along with Animal Home, the local veterinary hospital.

This university-accredited veterinary clinic featured four hours of surgery during which 30 animals, dogs and cats, were spayed or neutered. Event attendance exceeded expectations attracting over 200 participants, with 42 veterinary students and veterinarians on-site, and over 150 more joining via livestream.

This clinic event subsequently gained national notoriety via an article in the *United Spay Alliance Newsletter* that applauded the efforts of Spay Mexico and Spay Global to bring HQHVSN training directly into the veterinary curriculum of not one, but two, major universities. Further, it was heralded as an exciting advancement in the evolution of spay/neuter training—or, as Jeff would say and advocate, "Spaying it forward."

CHAPTER 6
DR. JEFF ROCKY MOUNTAIN VET

Maybe you've seen *Dr. Jeff Rocky Mountain Vet*, the top rated show on the Animal Planet television network from 2015-2021.

Its memorable and offbeat opening sequence with the Rocky Mountains near Denver, Colorado as a backdrop, led you into the life of maverick veterinarian Dr. Jeff Young and went like this:

... Cue the twangy guitar riff

... Show background scenes of the Colorado Rockies

Voiceover: "Denver, Colorado, home to one of America's busiest vets."

...Cue to city scenes of people and pets on the streets of Denver

...Cue to scenes inside the surgery room of Planned Pethood

Dr. Jeff's Voice – "Listen up! I need a tech."

Voiceover: "100,000 clients, a battle-hardened staff of 40, and a practice that knows no bounds. Dr. Jeff's challenge is keeping it all under control."

...Final cue to Dr. Jeff standing in front of PPI, arms crossed

Dr. Jeff's Voice – "This is me. This is what I love."

The show, ultimately a successful gamble for all involved, instantly

Animal Planet promotional poster

garnered Jeff a legion of fans of all ages who are still out there today as evidenced by his huge following on social media, including Facebook, Instagram, TikTok, and YouTube. The entire series is also available via subscription on the Discovery Plus network and for rental or purchase on Amazon Prime. Additionally, reruns of various episodes can be seen on the Discovery channel.

The show, a docuseries, also established Jeff as a bona fide television personality, and even today people still stop by the practice asking to meet him, pose for pictures, and tour the clinic.

Following the fan pages and postings, the number one comment is typically, "I really miss seeing your show," or, "When is the show coming back?"

As happens with television network programming, the Discovery Network, of which Animal Planet is a part, went through a complete change of personnel in 2020 and the executives involved with the *Dr. Jeff* show left to do other work. The decision was then made for the network to go in a different direction with streaming and subscription-based services rather than cable-based, as well as new programming, and the show was not renewed.

"When you get a turnover of people at a network," said Steve LuKanic, one of the *Dr. Jeff* show's producers (Seasons 4-8), "they often want to pursue new shows. It had nothing to do with Jeff; his popularity was, and is, still there."

The first question one might ask is, how did it all start? How did one veterinarian, popular and successful in his own right, come into the limelight of network television?

It all began in early 2015. The Planned Pethood practice on Tennyson Street in Denver was thriving, and everything was business as usual. That is until Jeff received a phone call that, unbeknownst to anyone, would take his life and his practice to another level and one that he never imagined.

That call came from Double Act Productions, a British television production company looking for a potential new reality show for Animal Planet. Having watched an impassioned speech from Jeff on YouTube about his spay/neuter platform and Street Dog Program, Double Act decided that a show about Jeff might fit the bill.

"I remember that phone call," recounted Jeff. "It came out of the blue and they were asking if I would be interested in doing a reality TV show. I knew about one such show on Animal Planet already, *Emergency Vets*, whose practice was also located in Denver."

Not quite sure what to make of the idea or if it was even a real offer, Jeff told Double Act, "I honestly don't know. I might be interested, but I don't know what's involved. You should know that I'm really very controversial and I'm not going to change my mind about how I do things or tone it down for any reason. You might want to check out my Facebook page and my website." Without much more to say, they said goodbye and Jeff went about his day not giving it any more thought.

That changed the next day, however, when Double Act called back and emphatically stated that they were indeed extremely interested in doing a show about Jeff and his practice. Further, they would be in town the following week to shoot some preliminary footage with Jeff if he was interested.

"It happened just that fast," recalled Jeff. "I don't think any of us thought that anything would really come of it. I didn't know how things were going to work out and I didn't see myself as a TV personality. I thought of it more like an adventure or an educational platform. I never looked at it from a financial standpoint."

When the Double Act film crew arrived from England the following week, the plan was to shoot a teaser, or "sizzle reel," a ten-to-twelve-minute video that would serve as a preview of the show. There was a problem from the outset, however, because there was no clear idea of what the show was going to be or what would be included in the teaser. So the film crew started following Jeff and his staff around for a couple of days at the Tennyson clinic and then to an off-site clinic in the mountains.

"None of us knew what was going to work," said Jeff. "To me it seemed as if there was a lot of wasted time and that they did an excessive amount of filming just to get ten or twelve minutes worth of material."

But Double Act was convinced that Animal Planet, not to mention viewers, would find the show appealing. And they were right. No sooner did Animal Planet watch the sizzle reel, they gave a greenlight to *Dr. Jeff Rocky Mountain Vet* and the show became an instant hit.

First and foremost viewers loved Jeff's compassion and care for animals in every situation, whether it was providing routine care, emergency care, or a complex case involving multiple issues. And that care included all sizes and types of animals—everything from companion pets to exotics and wildlife. The care for these animals, whether provided by Jeff or members of his staff, always involved Jeff's input and oversight.

Second, every animal was treated with the best of care and at an affordable price. Had it not been for Dr. Jeff, many of the people whose pets he treated might have had to consider euthanasia because they could not afford the necessary veterinary care elsewhere. With his low-cost services, and by maintaining a high-volume practice and a commitment to never turn away any animal in need, Jeff demonstrated and exemplified a much-needed and viable option so that all people could afford veterinary care for their animal.

Animal Planet promotional poster

Third, the show was educational. The filming brought viewers right into the surgery room as Jeff often sketched out the procedure he was about to perform on a white board, describing it in simple layman's terms, after which viewers watched the actual surgery. The show was also chock-full of information about other topics, including spay/neuter, vaccinations, pet adoption, and routine pet care. While the show was geared for an adult audience, it also inspired young people, even toddlers.

A perfect example of this was a three-year-old girl named Eliza who visited Planned Pethood with her grandmother. They had brought the family dog to the clinic for a check-up, but that wasn't the only item on Eliza's agenda. She kept telling her grandmother over and over that she really wanted to meet Dr. Jeff.

"Eliza watches the show all the time," her grandmother told the front desk staff who overheard Eliza's request.

"She can recite, verbatim, many parts of the show, like when Dr. Jeff is describing how he does a surgery. She tells us all the time that she wants to be a vet like Dr. Jeff when she grows up."

So at the end of their appointment, Jeff's daughter, Melody—the clinic's front desk manager—went back to the surgery area and told Jeff, "There's someone out here who would like to meet you."

Always obliging, Jeff walked out to the reception area and looked around to see who was waiting for him. He noticed the grandmother and walked towards her saying hello and extending his hand in welcome. The grandmother greeted Jeff and said, "I'm pleased to meet you, but this is the person who really wants to meet you, my granddaughter. She watches your show all the time."

Jeff, 6'3' in height, leaned down to shake hands with Eliza, a bit shorter, standing at about 2 ½ feet tall.

Eliza peered up at Jeff, wide-eyed, and said in a soft but firm voice, "When I grow up, I want to be a vet like you and fix animals."

"That's a very good thing," Jeff smiled. "I think you'll do that just fine."

Eliza's mission was accomplished. A brief encounter to be sure, but more importantly, a future veterinarian was in the making, and stories like this would happen throughout the show's run and long after.

Dr. Jeff Rocky Mountain Vet was relatable and inclusive in that viewers got a behind-the-scenes look at a real-life veterinary practice. All the stories told, from staff and pet owners alike, showed the heart, compassion, and emotion involved in the care and keeping of animals. It was a show where the stories kept unfolding and viewers wanted to see what happened to both the animals and the people involved.

In addition, viewers came to know the other veterinarians and staff at the clinic as well—Dr. Baier, Dr. Amy, Dr. Don, et al., adoption manager Susan, along with numerous vet staff and receptionists, including Hector and Melody, not to mention Jeff's wife and Head Surgeon, Dr. Petra. There were also student interns gaining valuable hands-on experience learning how to do spay/neuter surgeries and other procedures who were also featured on the show.

Then there were the out-of-clinic field trips where viewers went along for the ride to locations throughout Colorado, South Dakota, Mexico, Panama, and even Romania, and other settings that included Native American reservations, rural and isolated communities, and wildlife sanctuaries. During these trips, not only did Jeff treat domestic animals, but exotics of all kinds, including lions, tigers, bears, wolves, camels, llamas, monkeys, and alligators.

But perhaps the most inclusive and endearing story featured on the *Dr. Jeff* show throughout its eight seasons, was when Dr. Jeff shared his cancer diagnosis with the world at the end of Season 2. It was in this episode that Petra shaved off Jeff's signature long hair, falling out from initial chemotherapy treatments.

It was a heart-wrenching moment as staff gathered around Jeff who was seated on a chair in the middle of the surgery room. Palpable emotions of fear, concern, worry, and sadness filled the air.

During this episode, Hector Martinez, a vet tech on the show and Jeff's longtime friend, comments, "It ran through my mind that I could lose my best friend and it really does bother me. I told him, 'Jeff, I love you, I care about you very, very much. I'm always going to be by your side no matter what happens.'"

Melody, her face full of sadness, adds, "My dad has had long shaggy hair since I can remember. He always said that his hair is his strength and now he shaved it off."

Jeff, stoic and unemotional yet with a touch of weariness, maintains the same sense of courage and resiliency as when the cameras weren't rolling and says, "All you can do is make light of it. That's the point. I don't want people moping around. First off, they have no control over it, and I have no control over it. As for the hair, I would rather lose my hair than lose my life. It's weird having no hair but it will grow back. It's a small price to pay."

At the end of this episode, Jeff and Petra are shown heading upstairs to their apartment above the clinic. With their backs to the camera, Petra teasingly says to Jeff, "Can I shave my head, too?" To which Jeff nonchalantly replies, "Nope. I like your hair long."

"A huge reason for the popularity of the show," commented Steve Lu-Kanic, "was because Jeff told the network they could cover his bout with cancer. They had literally just signed him for Season 3 and had begun filming when he got this cancer diagnosis. The network was like, what do we do now? They came to Jeff and asked him if he wanted to take a hiatus or if he would be comfortable continuing to film the show, and Jeff said to keep the show going."

Steve added, "The episode people remember most was when Petra cut Jeff's hair. You could see the staff in the background crying because they knew how much his hair meant to him. I believe that moment cemented his popularity more than anything because people suddenly had this real guy, this vet who dedicated his life to helping other people and their pets, now

faced with his own life or death crisis. And what would that look like? So viewers became even more invested. They wanted to follow his journey."

Jeff summed it up by saying, "I feel like I've been blessed. I've stood on lots of mountaintops and scuba dived in lots of oceans. I've

*Jeff, scuba diving in
Cabo San Lucas, Mexico*

taught hundreds of veterinarians. Who could complain? A lot of people have it a lot worse than me. And even if I die from this, a lot of people have had it a lot worse than me their whole lives. Don't worry about me. I'm doing alright."

Right on the tail of the cancer diagnosis was yet another major event for Jeff and Planned Pethood.

In Season 2, after 24 years on Tennyson Street, Jeff moved the PPP practice to one nearly twice the size on Harlan Street in Wheat Ridge, about a mile and a half away. Here again Jeff and Petra would live above the clinic. It was a big move for the practice, and despite the days when his energy level was low due to chemo treatments, Jeff never missed a

*Helpers work with Jeff during
the move from the
Tennyson Street clinic to
the Harlan Street clinic*

day of work. The move became a reality through the additional help of staff and numerous volunteers, including members of his running team, friends, and family.

Remembering that time, Melody said, "My dad never took time off when he was fighting cancer. He slowed down physically because he was sick from the chemo. He would ask me to stop and get him some Yoo-hoo, a chocolate flavored drink, for breakfast in the mornings. That and regular chocolate milk were the only things he could tolerate and keep down. He was chugging chocolate milk and moving cages when we moved from Tennyson to Wheat Ridge. What kept him going was his passion for what he does."

As Season 3 progressed, and then into Season 4 in the fall of 2017, Jeff's cancer went into remission. As he predicted, his hair did grow back and, fortunately, he regained his vitality. Best of all, the practice was as busy as ever. The show, still number one on Animal Planet, with an average of 1.4 million viewers per episode, kept getting renewed. In the world of reality television, where one or two seasons is the average life span of a series, *Dr. Jeff Rocky Mountain Vet* was taking the market by storm and going way beyond the boundaries of what anyone had thought or expected, including Jeff.

"People ask me why I'm so popular," said Jeff. "I don't know. I think it's because we're real. It's really that simple in my mind. We're just real. We really do try to make a difference and we really believe in what we're doing."

For all its popularity, however, the show was a two-edged sword for Jeff. Whereas it gave him a worldwide platform to showcase his mission of providing affordable vet care along with the impact and importance of spay/neuter, the show also created numerous challenges for the practice.

"On Tennyson Street, before Animal Planet ever came along," Jeff said, "we already had 90,000 clients. When the show was filming, we still had to provide a service for those clients, even those who were never featured on the show. We were running a business and trying to film a television series at the same time and that wasn't easy."

The first season proved to be the most challenging for all concerned.

While the network was trying to lock down the format of the show and see where it fit in the market, Jeff and his staff were doing their best to accommodate. But, Jeff admits, the expectations of filming a reality television show were never fully explained or discussed with him or his staff, especially the time commitment involved.

During Season 1, for example, after a long day of veterinary work and filming, Jeff and his staff were often subject to lengthy interviews and voiceover recording sessions, not all of which were used in the show. This extra work often led to 10 to 12 hour days which frequently left Jeff and his staff exhausted.

While Season 1 may not have been quite what the doctor ordered, so to speak, the show immediately gained a foothold in the cable television market. Viewers really wanted to see more of

Opening and trailer images
for Season 1 of the show
Top photo: the Tennyson Street clinic
Bottom photo: L to R, Hector, Dyani,
Jeff, and Melody

this compassionate veterinarian who helped all animals, and at an affordable cost, and, now that Animal Planet had a hit TV show, it was immediately renewed for a second season.

For Season 2, Double Act brought producer Callie Zanandrie on board. Callie had been working on another veterinary show set in Alaska and she would become instrumental in finessing the production schedule and format of the *Dr. Jeff* show. Whereas the first season of the show focused mainly on Jeff's work at the Tennyson Street clinic, episodes in Season 2 would also include Jeff treating various exotic animal outside of the clinic.

"There was definitely a format for the show that Animal Planet wanted to follow," said Callie. "We would usually follow three to four animal stories at the clinic per episode, and those were mainly dogs, cats, reptiles, and birds. Sometimes we could deviate a little, but they also wanted the big story, an exotic animal of some kind involving a field trip where we would leave the clinic and Jeff would work on a horse, cow, pig, tiger, bear—you name it. And those field trips were my favorite. I loved being at the clinic, but it was a nice change of pace going on location."

All the animal stories on the show were true and the filming followed what happened as it happened. "Everything we filmed was organic," said Callie. "Nothing was made up or contrived."

"We were in the lobby every day scouting for stories," remarked Steve. "And the story of the animal was always the number one priority especially if it was unusual or we hadn't covered something like it before."

Steve added that it was just as important to cast the show based on the characteristics of the owners as much as the animal stories.

"We would look to see how articulate, how passionate, or how talkative the owners were and if they'd be willing to be on camera," said Steve. "We had people of all ages and from all walks of life. Little kids were especially fun to work with since they were so excited to be on TV."

"Some days," said Callie, "we would shoot six stories, some days nothing. It would just depend on what came through the door that day."

While the process of scouting for clinic stories was sometimes long and demanding, the producers and the staff became more and more adept at determining what made a good story and what didn't.

"And since it was often feast or famine," added Callie, "we always had a GoPro camera [live-streaming, high resolution, omnidirectional recording camera] fixed and rolling so that we could catch an emergency if it came through the front door."

Aside from daily filming, there was also follow-up filming for the ongoing thread-stories such as those involving orthopedic surgeries where healing occurred over time. "When we knew that we had to follow a thread-story," recounted Steve, "we would always check with Melody and the staff up front as to when these people were booking their follow-up appointments or if additional treatment was needed. We had to keep up so we could follow a story through to the end."

"I was so proud to work on the *Dr. Jeff* show," stated Steve, "because when I watched the shows after they were edited, especially the ones with long-term follow-up where peoples' pets were fully recovered, these animals were now healthy, happy, eating, and playing. It was the best thing because some of these animals had literally been at death's door when we met them. It was so rewarding to see their recovery, knowing it was a result of the care provided by Jeff and the team at Planned Pethood."

While filming clients and their pets was the main focus of the show, the other was filming the clinic staff while they were performing their daily jobs. From the front desk to the surgery room, nearly all personnel at the clinic were included in the filming of the show at some point. But not everyone on the staff enjoyed the filming process.

"The show drove me nuts!" exclaimed Melody. "We already had a tough situation trying to run a business and it can be a very difficult job, especially if there is an emergency. We didn't always have time to yell for the camera crew to start rolling. Sometimes the filming had to wait, and some of the crew understood that and some did not. But by the end of the series, though, I loved the whole crew."

"We knew and understood that we were working in a real business where they were treating real animals, and they had much bigger priorities than a television show," said Steve. "So it really became kind of a dance with Jeff and his staff. We had to give them the time, respect, and the freedom they needed to do their work, but at the same time we knew we had a mandate with the production company to produce a show."

Steve continued, "Sometimes that dance created conflict because Jeff would walk into the clinic and maybe Dr. Baier was out sick and one of the other vets was gone, and they had a slate of surgeries booked for the day and needed all hands on deck. And then here we were telling Jeff that he had to go with us to a wildlife sanctuary that day to film him neutering a tiger. That didn't make him too happy, considering his priority was to the clinic, even though he was contractually obligated to do the Animal Planet series as well."

The part of the show that weighed heaviest on Jeff came down to finances.

"Everybody thinks if you're on TV that you must be rich," said Jeff, "but from a financial standpoint, the show was a big challenge for us.

"For example, when one of the other doctors went with me on a trip, or maybe they went to an off-site location by themselves for a particular segment, I'd have one or two less doctors at the practice who were not treating animals and not making money for the clinic that day. This happened every season."

Another challenge that presented itself because of the show was an influx of clients from states outside of Colorado. These people, hearing of Jeff's affordable care on the show, took a chance and made their way to Planned Pethood, sometimes from as far away as the east coast.

"We actually had to stop taking out-of-state clients because of the follow-up care that was sometimes needed," said Jeff. "If an animal required a major surgery, for example, and the owner couldn't bring the pet back for follow-up visits, that was a disservice to both the animal and the owner."

Another anomaly of the show was that, per network mandates, cases involving the death of an animal, through natural causes or euthanasia, were rarely presented or discussed.

"That really bothered Jeff," said Steve, "because it made him look like he was this miracle worker who could save every animal that came his way. And that was not the case at all. There *were* times when an animal had to be put down for medical reasons, or when an animal didn't make it through a surgery, or it would be brought in for treatment and didn't survive."

In fact, it wasn't until the last season of the show when Jeff addressed the issue of losing a pet after a segment involving the death of vet tech Blair's dog during surgery.

"Death," said Jeff, "is a part of life. It's pretty common that we will outlive our pets, especially dogs. But I always tell people that they really have to take themselves out of the equation and not be selfish when it comes to the end of their pet's life. You may not want to let them go, but you'll know when they stop being themselves."

Jeff continued, "It's like with my dog Fred. I know who Fred is. I know when he likes to eat and I know when he loves to play. But when the day comes that Fred stops being Fred, I'll know that, too. I believe people know when their pets stop being themselves; animals will give signs. It's their way of saying, 'I've reached the end; you have to help me out here.'"

"It was so amazing to hear Jeff talk about this," commented Steve, "because every pet owner experiences the death of their pet at one time or another, and a lot of people, his fans, never knew Jeff's philosophy regarding euthanasia or the loss of an animal unless they happened to go through that experience at Planned Pethood. Nor did they know about Jeff's calm, sincere, and genuine bedside manner in that situation."

Steve continued, "Many times when we weren't filming, I would listen to Jeff talking with clients who lost a pet during surgery or one who died soon after being brought into the clinic. He is very personal and endearing and people naturally respond to him. He has really helped a lot of people through some very emotional experiences."

COVID Changes Everything – The Final Season

"We had just started filming Season 8 the first week of March 2020," said Steve, "when we began hearing about COVID and people started wearing masks. I think everyone on the crew and at the clinic was thinking, why are they wearing masks? How serious is this? We knew that COVID was in China and in Italy, but we didn't know it was in the United States yet.

"Then suddenly the NBA canceled its entire season and everyone started freaking out. And then came the shutdown. Although the clinic remained open, the TV crew was sent home because we weren't considered 'mandatory personnel.'"

In June of 2020, Animal Planet gave the okay for the show to resume production, although it was mandated that the entire crew and clinic staff had to wear masks at all times. The network wanted to show how Jeff and his clinic operated during a pandemic, something that had never before been documented.

The twelve episodes filmed during Season 8—nicknamed "The COVID Season" by the crew—wrapped production at the end of 2020.

"It was a tough season to film," remembered Steve. "We couldn't bring people into the clinic and there were times when Jeff had to go out to the parking lot and examine animals in cars. Not to mention, everyone had to wear masks which made it difficult to hear people, and Jeff's glasses were always fogging up during surgery!"

Still, Steve acknowledged that it was an interesting time because people were so appreciative of Jeff's presence and that he was still available to help their pets and perform surgeries as needed.

Season 8, the final season, had ten episodes. The last episode, which would turn out to be the series finale, was titled "Adoption Stories," and contained segments from the previous seven seasons as well as a behind-the-scenes look at how the show was produced, featuring the entire production crew.

After filming ended on Season 8, everyone wanted to hear when production would start up on Season 9; however, that's when Animal Planet decided not to renew the show.

 "It was disappointing knowing that the show wouldn't be back," said Steve, "because at that point, the crew, the staff—we were all like a family. Over time, Jeff had developed a trust with the crew and he knew how we operated. At the same time, we knew and respected Jeff's priorities and we allowed him to do his work while at the same time making a great TV show."

The Planned Pethood Staff at the Harlan Street clinic in Denver

For Jeff, the end of the *Dr. Jeff Rocky Mountain Vet* show was bitter-sweet in many ways.

"I knew it wouldn't go on forever," said Jeff, "but I was also aware of the impact the show had on people. For me, it was never about fame or fortune. I couldn't care less about that. The 'win' of the show for me was about educating and helping people and animals wherever there was a need. That was always my mission and it hasn't changed."

CHAPTER 7
ANIMAL TALES - THE DOMESTICS

At the Clinic – A Prelude

No two days are ever the same for Dr. Jeff and his staff at Planned Pethood. Whether he is in the Colorado clinic, on the road, stateside, or in another country, the variety and number of cases each day is remarkable. Some cases are routine, some are emergencies, and some are life or death. From the moment the doors open, no matter the place, clients are lined up, ready and waiting to bring in their animals.

It is 7 a.m. and already the reception area at the clinic is abuzz with activity and sound. Filling the air are the barks, meows, whimpers, and yips from animals of all shapes and sizes, along with lots of conversations as pet owners talk with clinic staff, each other, and their pets offering words of comfort to one another or sometimes reprimands to their pets as everyone is checked in and awaiting their consultation or exam time.

In the surgery area of the clinic, vet technicians and other staff are bustling back and forth prepping everything for the day. The technicians, a vital part of the animal care team, need to do several tasks before Jeff or the other veterinarians start their work, including checking on the animals who spent the night at the clinic, making sure each surgical area is stocked with packets of sterilized instruments and other supplies, running preliminary or follow-up testing on patients including x-rays or blood work, and helping to prep animals for surgery.

Soon, it is midday. Time has flown by, like a whirlwind, occasionally punctuated by a momentary lull during which Jeff calls out, "Okay everybody. Where's my next case? Is that FHO ready? Did the lab results I requested come in yet?" This is the nature of a high-volume clinic like Planned Pethood; a beehive of activity from the beginning of the day until those final moments at closing, and Jeff wouldn't have it any other way.

"Due to the high volume here," Jeff said, "there are tons more learning opportunities. One year here is like five years elsewhere because of all that we do. The best way for new vets to learn something is to do it. Around here, new vets get a lot of practice really fast."

As each work day stretches on, overtime often the norm, the staff remains until every animal that came into the clinic or worksite that day is attended to. Anyone who works with Jeff understands and follows his baseline principle that no animal needing help is turned away, no matter how severe the case, time of day, or the owner's ability to pay. Helping the animal is always the priority.

Although the work days can be long and tiring, staff members all agree that there is great satisfaction in being part of the Planned Pethood team. Still, it takes a bit of tenacity and humor to get through the longer days, as shown by one vet technician who quipped, "It's been ten hours since I've seen the sun. Is it still out there?!"

"That's Jeff's thing, helping animals until the day is done," said clinic manager Melody. "That's what Jeff talks about at our staff meetings. He says to us, 'I understand we're overbooked and sometimes we're overwhelmed, but any animal we send away when we're their last resort is an animal that will go home and die.' And I think that's what keeps him going because he knows he can prevent that from happening."

It's 11 p.m. and the clinic is now quiet on all fronts. If all the animals that visited that day could speak and were to say a closing word, one might hear a chorus of "thank yous!" to which Jeff would smile and reply, "You're welcome. Glad to be of service. It's all in a day's work and I'll be doing it again tomorrow."

Animal Tales - The Domestics

Following are a handful of cases with domestic animals, some featured on the *Dr. Jeff* show, that represent the breadth of Jeff's work and encompass his legacy of principles: quality, affordable veterinary care, spaying and neutering, community involvement and outreach, thinking globally and acting locally, saving rather than euthanizing, and not turning away any animal in need.

Fred, the Angel Dog: The Otherworldly vs. The Earthly

How does one here on the earthly plane counteract an otherworldly dictum concerning the treatment of a very sick dog when it is contrary to everything they know and believe?

If you're Jeff, you go with your gut and do what is best for the animal, no matter what it takes. And that sometimes plays out in the most unexpected way.

One such memorable story involved a three-year-old Golden Retriever who had stopped eating for two days and was constantly vomiting. Unsure of what the problem was, his owners brought him to Planned Pethood which happened to be near their home.

After examining and x-raying the dog, Jeff told them that surgery was needed to save their dog because he had swallowed what appeared to be a sock, and Jeff said he would do the surgery for $800. The couple hesitated and said they needed to "pray" on it and went out to the parking lot to confabulate. Meanwhile, their dog, in great distress, was still on

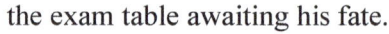

the exam table awaiting his fate.

Following their "prayer" time, the owners informed Jeff that God told them their dog did not need surgery. Jeff respectfully disagreed, stressing to them once again that without surgery the dog would die, and Jeff offered to reduce the price of the surgery even further.

Still hesitant, they said that additional consultation with God was needed and they returned to the parking lot once again. When they returned a short time later, they told Jeff that God had told them to euthanize their dog.

Now what?

Jeff knew for certain that a simple surgery could save this young, otherwise healthy dog, and that he could easily be adopted out through the Planned Pethood adoption center. Euthanasia was not necessary! So Jeff came up with Plan B: he offered to pay the couple a few hundred dollars to surrender their dog to him so he could save his life.

This time the owners did not hesitate. They took the cash and readily departed. A scam? Perhaps. But while some might believe that Jeff had been taken advantage of by simply trying to save this dog's life, he was about to get far more in return than he could have ever imagined.

Jeff quickly returned to the operating room where, in a short amount of time, he was able to remove the sock, complete the surgery, and feel confident that the dog would have smooth recovery.

That might have been the end of the story except for a couple of things that occurred in the interim. First, Jeff named the dog Fred and, as is often the case when someone names an animal, they started to become attached. Then, as Jeff watched Fred recover, an even stronger bond formed and the two of them kind of "fell" for one another. The same thing happened with Petra, and the next thing they knew, they had a dog of their very own, something that hadn't happened in quite a while. Jeff, Petra, and Fred became fast friends and started going everywhere together.

Now, looking back at that fateful day when Fred first arrived at the clinic, Jeff can't help but smile. "Fred is incredible," said Jeff. "He's one of the best dogs I've ever had."

Fred's special domain, though, is at the clinic where he watches over everything, as if on guard duty, much like one would expect of a guardian angel. At various times during the day, Fred makes rounds throughout the clinic, stopping by each cage or each animal recovering from anesthesia, as if checking on them and offering comfort, and then he also visits the staff to see who might be available to provide a treat or a little TLC.

Sometimes, when either Jeff or Petra is performing a difficult surgery, Fred remains by their side until it is completed. At other times, he assumes a resting sentry-type post by lying down in the middle of the floor, apparently unobserving, but with eyes half-masted, watching everything going on around him, still on guard duty. Fred is what you might call an "angel of a dog" and he is loved by everyone at the clinic, especially Jeff and Petra.

Fred, although older now, is still going strong. Without a doubt, though, Jeff's conviction of saving an animal rather than letting it die, helped him to countermand an otherworldly message that made all the difference in *this* world for a Golden Retriever named Fred.

A Dog, a Homeless Man, and a Debt Repaid

A man named Adrian walked into the Planned Pethood clinic cradling Kyara, a 5 ½ month old dog, in his arms. "I hope you can help me. My dog has a busted paw," Adrian told the receptionist. "She jumped off of something high and landed funny."

In the consultation room, as Jeff started to examine the dog, Adrian spoke up saying, "I'm homeless and I don't have a whole lot of money to pay for this. I don't want to have to put her to sleep because I can't pay much for surgery if it is needed. I love this dog! She's not just a dog to me but a friend; a better friend than a lot of two-legged people."

"My goal," Jeff explained to Adrian, "is to get this dog back in your arms. Let's do some x-rays and see what's needed." The x-rays revealed multiple breaks in one paw that required surgical intervention if the dog was ever going to have use of that leg again. In the back of his mind, Jeff hoped that Adrian, homeless and a wanderer, would be able to maintain the care needed for the dog over time, particularly since a series of follow-ups would be required as the leg healed from surgery.

"I'll do the surgery for $100," Jeff told Adrian, "and you can pay me back when you can." Adrian solemnly promised that he would pay the charge.

From experience, Jeff understood the psychological principle involved with charging for a procedure versus doing it at no cost. If a value is not placed on the animal by charging for the service provided, then the animal is not valued by the owner, and follow-up care is often deemed negligible. Further, Jeff knew that people like to be treated with respect, and that even those with little or no income want to give something in return for something received. The overriding concern for Jeff though, was not payment; it was to fix the dog's broken leg and reunite the man with his beloved companion.

For several days, Adrian and Kyara were apart while surgery and initial post operative care took place. During that time, Adrian was lonely without her and, when he came to pick her up after the successful surgery and recovery, he told a Planned Pethood staff member, "I didn't know what to do without Kyara. I can't wait to get her back. Before I got her, I was crazy, just wandering. She means a lot to me. We travel a lot. I don't talk to many people. Having her as my companion, I now have someone to talk to and share things with."

Adrian, so happy that he did not have to euthanize Kyara and to have her back with him, carefully followed all the post operative care instructions and brought the dog in every two weeks for follow-up visits as required. After several weeks, Kyara made a complete recovery and returned to being a playful, energetic young puppy.

The story does not end here though. There was still the matter of payment, and Adrian did not forget nor renege on his promise. Week by week, every time Adrian had a few extra dollars, he came to the clinic and paid down his bill, little by little, until the debt was paid in full. When the final payment was made, Jeff shook Adrian's hand and said, "Thanks for paying me. There are rich people who never pay me, but you did."

Reflecting on this case, Jeff noted, "Adrian really worked closely with his dog. He truly cares about her. He didn't give up on her or give her to a shelter. I can make the argument that Kyara is better off with Adrian than a lot of dogs in richer neighborhoods." The story of Adrian and Kyara is one of the many cases in which Jeff made quality, affordable veterinary care available to another person, no matter their income.

The Days of Spay and Neuter – Here, There, and Everywhere

From the very beginning of his veterinary career, Jeff has been a relentless advocate for spaying and neutering to control overpopulation to avoid what he calls "senseless" euthanasia. He even started his career with a mobile spay/neuter bus traveling throughout Colorado and the western United States wherever there was a need.

These days, while the mobile clinic is no longer, Jeff continues to travel on weekends or multiple day jaunts, offering low-cost spay/neuter services here, there, and everywhere, from communities in remote locales, to those in low-income or impoverished areas with no access to veterinary care, including Native American reservations and other locations throughout the world.

Offering his services outside of the clinic setting is the basis for Jeff's philosophy of both community outreach and thinking globally and acting locally. While doing these spay/neuter clinics often makes for long weeks, with very little down time, it is also very much in keeping with Jeff's energy level and his belief in the precept of paying it forward, or "spaying" it forward as he says, and giving back to the community at large.

Jeff framed it like this: "This is what I cut my teeth on, mobile spay/neuter clinics. I will definitely do this until the day I die. I try to go where there is the greatest need. I do the best I can and hopefully, in some small way, I can change or help a small part of the world." Incidentally, to date Jeff has performed spay/neuter on over 200,000 animals.

Underlying all of Jeff's work is his understanding of and appreciation for the animal/human bond. "The truth is," said Jeff, "many of these pets are like members of the family to their owners. They really care about their animals, and that's what matters to me. I will always try to help those who care about animals."

When conducting spay/neuter events at locations outside of the clinic, Jeff enlists numerous volunteers to help, including veterinarians, vet technicians, and others to assist with miscellaneous tasks. Most of these events are done gratis with all staff and workers donating their time. In some areas, such as the Native American reservations or areas where the Street Dog Program to control animal overpopulation has been adopted, the spay/neuter events are sometimes subsidized in part by outside funding and donations to help cover operating expenses.

While the primary reason for the off-site clinics is spay/neuter, people also bring their pets in for emergencies and other veterinary care: porcupine quills in a dog's snout, removal of masses or lumps, wounds of all types, skin issues...the list goes on. Many of these extra cases can be handled at the event site depending on the seriousness of the problem and if the proper equipment is on hand.

There are cases, though, that cannot be handled at the site due to the complexity of the problem, such as broken bones or joints, and other conditions. In these cases, Jeff has been known to bring a relinquished animal or two back with him to Planned Pethood for surgery, rehabilitation, and adoption. Or, depending on the locale and individual situation, sometimes the owner travels to Planned Pethood to pick up their pet after a surgery and post operative recovery time.

The impact of these clinics is not without measure and extends beyond just the number of animals helped to include many forms of appreciation and respect shown to Jeff and his team: words of thanks, special prayers, handmade gifts, and most of all, attitude and cultural changes leading to better care and treatment of animals.

Stories from the Spay/Neuter Sites

The Site: Eckley, Colorado, population 250, a town with no veterinarian and the nearest veterinary clinic is 100 miles away

Hope, a two-month-old rescued kitten with a hernia 1/3 the size of her tiny body. Although no one knew if the hernia was traumatic or congenital, the fact was that Hope's intestines were exposed and she would not live unless something was done.

Hope's rescuer, Donna, said, "Although I've only had her for a week, I've fallen in love with this cat and I hope she can be saved. That's why I named her Hope."

After examining Hope, Jeff confirmed that surgery was necessary for the kitten to survive. "Because she's so small, it will be a tough surgery," Jeff said. "I don't know if there's enough tissue to work with to close. There's no guarantee, but I'll do my best to try and save her. I'll also spay her to make sure that's taken care of just in case."

The surgery was touch-and-go as Jeff struggled to close the hernia on this kitten who, being so young and small, had very little extra skin with which to work. Finally, though, the hernial wound was closed and the surgery completed. Hope now needed to be quickly warmed and given fluids as she began the road to recovery. While the surgery appeared successful, only time would tell if the hernia would heal and remain closed.

The good news is that, after several weeks, Hope thoroughly recovered and became a thriving, playful kitten—also now spayed and ready to live fully. Donna, overjoyed to have Hope in her life for certain, could not say thank you enough to Jeff for not giving up on Hope and saving her life.

The Site: The Rosebud Lakota Sioux Reservation
in Mission, South Dakota

The spay/neuter clinic was just about ready to begin when suddenly a loud voice broke through the air saying, in Lakota, "*Aho! Hiyu wo oyate!*" which translates to "*Hello! Come, people!*" in English.

With the Lakota tribe, it is first things first, and, before any special event begins, a prayer is given by the tribe leader. The Planned Pethood staff and volunteers, along with the tribe elders leading the event, all gathered to form a circle with the leader standing in the center of the circle.

The leader began to chant, in Lakota, a prayer addressed to the Great Spirit. The prayer, honoring the interconnectedness of all life, asked for blessings on the people that came to help the animals, along with continued good health and well-being for all the animals of the tribe. The prayer was a gift of respect and honor to Jeff and his team in recognition of their work on the reservation. Now the clinic could begin and there was already a long line of patients.

One of the cases at the reservation involved a young German Shepherd, Bailey, who not only needed to be neutered but who also had an unusual mass on his side that had been present for several months. The dog's owner, Keith, said that Bailey didn't appear to be in any pain, but he was concerned and wanted to have it checked out.

Ultimately, Jeff determined that the mass was benign and removed it. Keith, glad that Bailey was finally neutered and that the mass was gone, looked forward to playing with his dog again. Keith commented, "I'm very grateful and humbled that someone from the city would care that much about us and come all the way here to help."

At the end of the day, the tribe leader once again called for a gathering to offer a parting prayer of thanks. After the prayer, a woman of the tribe touched Jeff's arm and asked him to wait a moment.

Reaching into her shoulder bag, she took out a beaded necklace and placed it in Jeff's hands. Continuing to hold her hands over his, she said, "This is a gift from the tribe. We know that you are struggling with cancer. This handmade necklace is a healing talisman for you so that you will heal from the cancer."

Jeff, honored and overwhelmed, accepted the necklace with a bow of his head and murmured a humble thank you.

Other Unforgettable Tales

The Romanian Brigade – An International Street Dog Tale

A case of note from a trip to Romania involved an older street dog brought to a shelter with multiple severe viral tumors and infected abscesses in one of its ears that also caused a loss of hearing. At first glance, the ear looked irreparable and other people at the shelter wondered if the dog was worth saving. Jeff saw and knew something different. The dog, while older and a mutt, was still in good health, friendly, and with the right treatment probably had a good chance of being adopted.

Whereas the shelter was ready to turn the dog away, even considering euthanasia, Jeff wasn't about to give up. He said, "Giving up is not in my dictionary," and promptly proceeded to operate on the infected ear.

It took a while, but with the tumors and abscesses removed, and the infection cleaned out, the dog regained partial hearing and the ear began to heal. The effort was a success on all fronts when soon afterwards the dog was indeed adopted.

The example set by Jeff in this case, to first look for the possibilities to help and rehabilitate, had a profound impact on the personnel at the shelter. As part of their new protocol, they continue to work closely with their local veterinarians to try and save the animal first before considering euthanasia.

National Mill Dog Rescue Program Tale – Lily's First Bed

For many years, Jeff has worked with Theresa Strader, Executive Director and Founder of National Mill Dog Rescue (NMDR) in Peyton, Colorado, to help spay/neuter and provide veterinary care to dogs rescued from breeding mills. Since 2007, NMDR has adopted out more than 18,000 dogs rescued from mills, 100% of which are spayed or neutered prior to adoption.

"These mills," said Jeff, "are mass production of so-called pure-bred dogs, most of which are kept in horrible conditions. When they reach a certain age, get sick, or they're no longer cute enough, they're killed or given away. If not for Theresa, these dogs would be dead."

One trip in 2017 had Jeff traveling to NMDR with assistant Hector and adoption manager Susan Rieger to assess and help with the latest group of rescued dogs as well as attending to several dogs already at NMDR.

After greeting one another, Theresa, Jeff, and the team walked over to the NMDR van. As they opened the vehicle door, they saw the most recent group of rescue dogs, 28 in total, staring out at them with looks ranging from blankness to fear. Each dog was in a separate carrier cage, many cowering at the back of their enclosures. It was oddly quiet.

Opening the door of one cage, Hector gently picked up a one-eyed dog. Instantly the dog began peddling all four legs, mechanically, like a wound-up toy. Theresa said, "They do that when they've never been held or picked up—when they've always been on a leash. They're trying to put their feet down on something because right now there is nothing for them to stand on."

Theresa's focus was on Lily, a raggedy looking 11-year-old Westie with numerous sores over her body and who was, until this rescue, still being bred. Lily also had an ulcerated eye and severely cracked paw pads. Taking Lily inside to the facility, Theresa and Susan bathed her and discovered that the sores were extensive, having penetrated beneath the fur to the skin, and covered almost all of Lily's body. They called Jeff in to take a look.

"She has severe skin allergies that have never been attended to," said Jeff, visibly frustrated. "This will take a while to heal. Using a mild astringent shampoo will help. For the paws, soak them in Betadine. Since she won't be standing on wire anymore, that will help a lot to get them healed."

Lily, now bathed and ready for stage one of rehab, was placed in a relatively large open area, measuring nine square feet surrounded by a low two-foot fence. Theresa and Susan watched as Lily tottered around this new space, much larger than anything she had ever known. Gone was the wire caging beneath her feet, now replaced by solid flooring. Gone was the leash around her neck holding her in short reign.

On one side of the area was, for her, a foreign object that she walked over to and sniffed with hesitant interest. She walked around the object twice and then just sat, staring. After several minutes, she got up and gingerly stepped into the object, a soft, sherpa-covered dog bed. She stood still for a few long moments and then finally laid down and closed her eyes. The simple comfort of a soft bed was something she had never known until now.

Tears were streaming down Theresa's face as she looked at Susan and said, "That's why we do our rescue work."

Meanwhile, in the clinical area of NMDR, Jeff performed several spay/neuter procedures on those animals already at the facility and provided additional care as needed for several other dogs.

During one spay of a three-year-old English Bulldog, Jeff and Hector noticed extensive scarring and fragile tissue on the dog's underside, causing difficulty for this usually routine procedure. It became apparent that the dog had multiple surgeries, c-sections, over the years.

"With multiple c-sections there's a lot of scarring and the tissue breaks down," commented Jeff. "Areas that are not supposed to be bleeding are bleeding. This dog is young to have so much scar tissue." Soon though, despite some difficult moments, the spay was completed successfully and the bulldog would, after a brief rehab, be ready for adoption.

As Jeff and his team prepared to leave NMDR at the end of the day, hugs and words of thanks were exchanged. Both Jeff and Theresa remain committed to the same cause: helping and saving animals.

"Jeff and I are kindred spirits where animals are concerned," said Theresa. "Animals first, always—their well-being, their care, and getting them spayed and neutered so they can live longer, healthier lives and not be unnecessarily reproducing."

"Theresa is a saint in my mind," said Jeff. "She is a really good human being who cares about animals, and I will always try and help people who care about animals."

Rocky, The Pit Bull vs. the Rattlesnake – Bite vs. Might

One night, Rocky, a three-year-old Pit Bull, was bitten on the leg by something, likely a rattlesnake. His owners tried to tend to it themselves but the next day, when Rocky's wound was considerably more swollen and inflamed, they took him to a local veterinarian who wanted $2,000 to be of service. Not having that amount of money, and wanting to save their family pet, they sought other avenues and were referred to PPI.

The entire family of five—mom, dad, and their three kids—filed into the clinic with Rocky in the dad's arms. The youngest child, a boy, was in tears and asked if Rocky was going to die. His mother, equally tearful, soothed her son with the words, "They're not going to let Rocky die." Her words, while hopeful, belied the doubt in her eyes because, in truth, no one knew for sure what was going to happen.

Jeff wasted no time in assessing Rocky's wound and went out to the lobby to discuss the situation with the owners. He informed them that although he had no antivenom, it wouldn't make a difference since the antivenom needed to be administered within 24 hours of the bite. Jeff also admitted that he had never seen a bite like this one and wasn't sure how or if Rocky would recover or if he might need his leg amputated. True to form though, Jeff offered to do his best for a reasonable fee, and the owners left Rocky in his care.

Over the next few days, Jeff did everything he knew to help Rocky. First, he placed the dog on IV fluids while also administering steroids and antibiotics to help lessen the effect of the venom. Second, he got Rocky on the operating table and made a few cuts to drain the burgeoning wound that relieved the pressure and allowed for better blood flow. He wrapped the wound loosely and waited. Amazingly, Rocky was calm and cooperative throughout all the procedures with only a few whimpers of pain.

The next day, the swelling was down and Jeff cut away some of the tissue deadened by the venom and sutured the wound loosely. At this point, about 72 hours from the incident, Jeff was pretty sure Rocky was going to live, but not 100% sure if he was going to lose his leg. Whereas a lot of surface damage was visible, it was difficult to know exactly how deep the venom had penetrated and what other damage was sustained. Only time would tell what else needed to be done.

Four days later, the wound on Rocky's leg was almost closed and Jeff placed new sutures to secure the closure. The prognosis for recovery looked good, and now it was time to return Rocky to his family and see how the wound healed over time.

It was a happy day for Rocky and his family when, a few weeks later, a follow-up exam revealed that his leg was totally healed and no amputation was necessary. Rocky was back to his normal self, romping and playing out in the yard with all the kids.

Interestingly, the family never found or saw the snake in their yard.

Reflecting on the case and Rocky's healing, Jeff didn't want to take the credit and said, "It was really Rocky more than me. He is one tough dog." Truth be told, however, saving Rocky's life was a dual effort: Jeff's affordable care and refusal to give up, and Rocky's internal strength, his GRRR factor. One helped the other because neither gave up.

Peanut the Australian Shepherd – Battle with a Rare Disease

Rachael and her two daughters knew something was wrong when Peanut, the family's 11-year-old Australian Shepherd, whom they had since she was a puppy, wandered off and disappeared. For five days, Rachael and her daughters searched for Peanut until they found her, collapsed in the snow, in someone's front yard 25 miles away.

Rushing Peanut to their local vet, the family discovered that Peanut had a challenging problem: a rare thyroid tumor on her neck that, if not surgically removed, would cause Peanut's death. Before being referred to PPI, Rachael had received quotes of up to $6,000 for the surgery.

With tears in her eyes, Rachael said, "It's one thing when you know there's nothing you can do, but it's another thing when you know there's something you can do but it's not within your reach." The family desperately wanted to save Peanut, so they came to PPI, their last and only hope for a quality and affordable option to save their beloved dog.

On this case, Jeff commented, "I believe in health care for all humans, and when animals become part of our family, they're entitled to a certain amount of health care, too. No one should have to go into debt to take care of their pets."

Offering to do the surgery for significantly less, Jeff first took x-rays to determine whether the cancer had spread to the lungs or other areas. If it had, then removing the thyroid tumor wouldn't help. Luckily, the cancer hadn't spread to any other area so surgery was a viable option.

Removing this type of tumor, a first for Jeff, was a bit challenging due to its location on the neck, a very vascular area that often causes excessive bleeding during surgery. With continued good fortune, though, the surgery proceeded without complications.

"This is as good as it gets," Jeff said after the surgery. "The tumor was not attached and it came out easily. Peanut now has some good years left. She's one for the record books."

Two days after the surgery, Rachael came to the clinic to pick Peanut up and take her home. "My daughters had to be at school today," Rachael told Jeff, "so they sent letters to you telling how grateful we are that you saved our Peanut." She handed the letters to Jeff who then posted them on the clinic bulletin board. The letters, each handwritten with crayon and featuring drawings of Peanut and a stick figure Jeff read, "Thank you for saving Peanut!"

A few weeks later, Peanut was back to her normal self and the family would go on to cherish every minute spent with their beloved furry family member. "My daughters think Dr. Jeff is a miracle vet!" smiled Rachael. "We knew it was not her time to go and now she will live to celebrate her next birthday and hopefully many more. Dr. Jeff helped make that possible. It's a wonderful life with Peanut here."

While Peanut's case, a battle against a rare, life-threatening disease was the first of its kind for Jeff at the time, it certainly wasn't his last. He continually wins battles as such with dogged determination, a willingness to try and not give up, and to offer quality affordable care for animals that are part of a family. Helping people and their animals...that's Jeff, doing what he loves.

No Animal Turned Away – Saving the Cat that Saved Its Owner, A Vet Tech's Tale

From day one, Courtney Morris, a vet technician with Planned Pethood from 2006-2014, was totally sold on Jeff's mission to help people obtain veterinary care at affordable prices and promote the cause of spay/

neuter while teaching other vets how to do it efficiently. What she also discovered was that Jeff's service extended way beyond the more traditional boundaries of animal care and service when she saw first-hand how no animal in need was turned away.

"The most memorable case for me," recalled Courtney, "was the time that Planned Pethood received a call, very near closing time, from Animal Control in Arvada, Colorado asking if we could help with a cat they had confiscated from a domestic violence crime scene. The cat, who had been trying to protect her owner and her litter of kittens, had been stomped on and stabbed several times by the woman's abusive partner.

"This mama cat was in very, very bad shape. They didn't know if she could be saved or if she would even survive all the wounds. There were also several kittens who were, thankfully, unharmed. Despite the late hour of the day, and not even asking about payment, Jeff immediately told them to bring the cats in.

"That day happened to be one of the times that Dr. Tony from Mexico was visiting, so Jeff and Tony got together and proceeded to spend the next four hours fixing every cut, stab wound, and hernia on this mama cat. We didn't have a ventilator, so I had to hand-ventilate for this cat while she was under anesthesia."

Courtney continued, "Afterwards, over many days, we nursed the cat back to health and found homes for her and all the kittens. If I remember correctly, the woman never received a bill for anything. Incidentally, the woman eventually got back to a safe place and her partner was actually convicted of both a felony *and* animal cruelty. A lot of times people never get fully prosecuted for animal cruelty charges, but it happened in this case."

In a final reflection, Courtney said, "That was one of the great things about working at Planned Pethood. I have worked at other clinics where people will just say, 'we're closed' when a complicated or difficult case comes along. Not Jeff! He will take any animal in at any time and help anybody. I will never forget how Jeff and Tony helped that cat—not turning her away or letting her die just because she was a case that came in after hours."

Nova, the Bernese Mountain Dog - Lost, Found, and Saved

Dr. Jeff's reputation and notoriety for compassionate and affordable veterinary care, long since established and aided along the way by the *Dr. Jeff Rocky Mountain Vet* show, was once again in the spotlight in December 2023 when Nova, a dog with a shattered leg, was brought to the clinic. Not only had Nova's owner had another of her animals helped by Jeff a few decades prior, but Nova's story went national with an article published in the *New York Post* titled, "TV Vet Saves 'Shattered' Leg of Dog Who Survived in Colorado Mountains for Two Months."

Here is a retelling of that national news story about Nova and Jeff's involvement...

One fall day, Nova, a young Bernese Mountain service dog in training, was so inexplicably spooked that she bolted and slipped out of her harness. Scared and alarmed, the only thing on Nova's mind was to run, and run she did, straight into the mountain wilderness of Conifer. She soon became lost in a cold, alien environment that was very dangerous for the likes of a domesticated dog.

Nova's owner, Robynne Simons-Sealy, was filled with despair at the loss of her service dog to help her through her seizure-type bouts from a rare disease called Takayasu arteritis. The search continued for several days but Nova was nowhere to be found. Weeks passed and Robynne had given up hope that she would ever see her dog again.

Two months later, everything changed when Robynne received word that two hikers had found Nova high atop a mountain trail hiding under some tree brush. Nova, acutely traumatized, also had one badly shattered leg.

Ecstatic to be reunited with her dog, Robynne also knew that saving Nova's leg would require skilled veterinary care and surgery. Robynne first took Nova to an emergency veterinary clinic where she received the disconcerting news that Nova's leg was "beyond repair" and amputation was the recommended course of action. Believing in her heart that the leg could be repaired, and unwilling to consider amputation as the only alternative, Robynne then took Nova to a few other veterinarians whose surgery prices to fix the leg ranged from $10,000 to $15,000. The cost—unaffordable to say the least—was always accompanied by an even stronger recommendation that amputation, not surgery, was the "better" and more affordable solution.

Still resolute that Nova's leg could be fixed, Robynne continued her search and finally landed at Planned Pethood International (PPI), a clinic that she could afford and, more importantly, a veterinarian who said, "Let's try and save that leg first rather than amputate."

During Nova's consultation at PPI, it dawned on Robynne that the clinic's owner, Dr. Jeff Young, was the same veterinarian who, a few decades earlier, had worked on one of her other dogs with great success. In that moment she knew that she could trust Jeff to help save Nova's leg.

"So many times," said Jeff, "dogs lose their limbs for financial reasons. For a lot of veterinarians, it's about the money. They will say they can fix the leg for $5,000 to $10,000 or cut it off for $1,000 to $2,000. In my mind, Nova's case was, honestly, a simple fix. I never would have recommended amputation in this case. My goal is always to give it my best shot to save the limb first, even if it's really bad."

Nova's leg, broken in several places, required six pins and two external bars to hold the reconstructed leg in place until it healed. The complex surgery was successfully completed by both Jeff and Dr. Petra, although Jeff wholeheartedly credited Petra for its ultimate success due to her extensive expertise and skill with bone surgery.

The day after the surgery, as he watched Nova romp around the recovery area at the clinic with her tail wagging a mile a minute, Jeff said, "She's walking on that leg today and even jumping. I would prefer she didn't, but the surgery repair is virtually 'bombproof' and it will heal fully in about two to three months."

Today, Nova remains a healed, healthy, four-legged dog. Whereas only time will tell if she will overcome her wilderness trauma to become the fully attentive service dog needed by her owner, Nova assuredly has all the physical potential needed, thanks to Drs. Jeff and Petra—veterinarians doing their utmost to do what's best for an animal at an affordable price.

CHAPTER 8
ANIMAL TALES - THE EXOTICS

All kinds of animals! While the primary focus of Dr. Jeff's veterinary practice has long been on dogs and cats, his quest to help animals in need has sometimes led him beyond the boundaries to work with a myriad of other animals.

The list of exotic animal encounters expanded greatly during the run of the *Dr. Jeff Rocky Mountain Vet* show where each show featured a trip to a location outside the clinic setting. During these episodes, Jeff found himself working on animals that he never dreamed of, including lions, tigers, bears, llamas, bison, jaguars, alligators, and a host of others.

With exotics and wildlife, sometimes the tasks are known ahead of time, such as with sessions scheduled at sanctuaries, or those involving large animals where sedation is required along with other professionals on hand to assist. Other times, the daily agenda is whatever case presents itself, especially during road trip clinics to remote areas that have little or no access to veterinary care. As in the clinic setting though, Jeff's job is keeping it all under control and to be prepared for anything.

To follow is a reprise of the most memorable exotic animal tales from both Jeff's road trip experiences and those from the television show.

A Road Trip, a Surprise, and a New Venture

"We're going to do a mobile clinic run this weekend," called out Jeff to his staff. "Who wants to go along?"

Chattering immediately rippled through the air as everyone, excited by the prospect of working outside of the clinic, each started vying for a turn to go on the trip. Never mind that road trips were done gratis and their time is volunteered. The fact was that road trips always proved to be great adventures and everyone at the clinic always wanted a chance to participate. This Saturday jaunt would take them to Leadville, Colorado, 100 miles west of Denver, one of the highest cities in America situated at the 10,000-foot elevation mark in the Rocky Mountains.

Contributing to the adventure aspect of this trip was the addition of several new people accompanying the clinical team. These newcomers, the film crew on the *Dr. Jeff Rocky Mountain Vet* show, were tasked with filming this trip that would be a part of the very first episode.

On the drive to Leadville, Jeff talked to his team about the work to be done and the day ahead. "These smaller communities really need outreach for animal care," Jeff reminded everyone. "Many of them just don't have the finances to get basic health care for their animals, and that's what we provide. I love coming up here. You never know what you're going to see or what animals you're going to be asked to work on which kind of makes it fun and exciting."

Arriving at the temporary clinic site, the team set up in a cabin owned by Jeff's friends from the Leadville animal shelter. When word got out that Jeff's mobile clinic had arrived, the locals started filing in with their pets of all shapes and sizes. It all looked like pretty normal fare for this area—dogs, cats, a chicken, a goat, a pet turtle—with routine needs like spay/neuter, abscess removal, and vaccines until a camel named Sullivan sauntered up to check in with his owner walking alongside.

The staff, momentarily astonished, quickly recovered at the sight of this extremely well-groomed, seven-foot tall, two-humped white bull camel, one and a half years young and about 500 pounds. A camel in the mountains of Colorado? What on earth was he doing there? Quite simply, Sullivan needed to be gelded to prevent unwanted mating.

The only one who did not show any surprise by Sullivan's appearance was Jeff. In fact, although he had never been up close to a camel, much less neutered one, Jeff simply walked right up to Sullivan, petted him, and talked quietly to him mentally assessing his patient's temperament and physique. Jeff was undaunted at the task of neutering this large, unfamiliar animal.

"I've neutered lots of bulls and even a llama recently," remarked Jeff with confidence to the camera for the benefit of his future viewing audience. "They're all about the same."

Since the operating area inside the cabin could not accommodate a large animal like Sullivan, a blanketed surface was prepared in a nearby clearing on which the surgery would be performed.

"Camels are sensitive to anesthesia," explained Jeff to his assistants, "so the most we use will be one quarter of what we give a horse. He won't be fully sedated, so we'll have to be fairly quick about this."

As the sedative started to take effect and Sullivan softly tumbled to the ground, a blanket was wrapped around his eyes while his feet were tucked under his frame to help prevent any reflexive kicks. Seated on the ground, Hector held Sullivan's head against his chest while a vet tech wrapped his arms around Sullivan's neck. Yet another tech prepared to assist Jeff as he began the surgery.

"His testicles are really slimy," muttered Jeff aloud as he struggled to be quick and efficient. Continuing to talk as he worked, Jeff expressed his concern about the anesthesia.

"The reality is that I really don't want to give him any more anesthesia. I want to get this done. If he decides to get up suddenly and give us a kick, you can imagine how that would feel."

Meanwhile, Hector, feeling the weight of Sullivan's head on his body, and sensing some movement from the camel, wondered how much longer the anesthesia would last and called to Jeff, "You really need to pick up the pace, man!"

Jeff, seemingly not hearing Hector's comment, maintained his concentration and said decidedly, "I'm going to open this incision up a bit more." A few minutes later, the testicles slipped out and Jeff snipped them off.

"That's it, we're done!" Jeff announced to everyone's relief as he closed the incision with quick precision.

Soon after Sullivan's surgery, the last task of the day at the Leadville site, the sun was beginning to set on the mountainside. Jeff stood nearby and watched as Sullivan awakened from the anesthesia and stood up tall after a few wobbly steps. Now alert and seemingly unfazed by the proceedings, Sullivan was tethered and led back to the trailer for the ride home. When the owner and animal walked by Jeff, the owner waved and said "Thank you!" while Sullivan simply walked by without a glance either way.

As this mobile clinic day came to an end, Jeff took a moment to reflect.

Turning to face the camera, he smiled easily and remarked, "I really love helping people out here. This was a pretty cool day and now it's time to get back to the clinic."

A Celebrity Named Larry

Meet Larry, the second camel who came into Jeff's life unexpectedly. He's a one-humped rescue camel who lives alongside several horses on

the Aurin family farm near Steamboat Springs, Colorado. A local celebrity with a smooth walk, a lazy grin, and his own blog, Larry is best-known for his annual appearances in the Steamboat Springs Fourth of July parades.

Turns out, Larry had a special friend named Camille, a two-humped rescue camel brought to the Aurin

Larry, the camel

farm as an intended mate for Larry with the hopes of having a camel calf or two. Would it be love at first sight?

Unfortunately, no. Larry and Camille did not hit it off. Mere tolerance was the attitude at their first meeting and, alas, despite repeated encounters of the dating kind over a long period, there was not even an iota of a spark between the two camels.

Unrequited in terms of a mate, Larry's personality started changing and he became increasingly cranky, temperamental, and aggressive. The Aurins knew, from raising horses, that unruly males often become calmer and more amicable after neutering. So, with no camel calves in the future, and to help Larry regain his former demeanor, the Aurins decided it was time for Larry to be neutered.

But who would do the job? Finding someone to neuter a large, exotic animal proved challenging. The Aurins called numerous professionals all over the state of Colorado, including the Colorado State University vet school, the Denver Zoo, and other exotic animal vets, but none had ever neutered a camel.

Finally, Mrs. Aurin—having known about Jeff from watching the Animal Planet television series which often featured exotic animals and unusual vet service requests—called Planned Pethood. While the Aurins had not seen the episode where Jeff neutered his first camel, Sullivan, they were thrilled to learn that he indeed had the experience they were seeking to neuter Larry and knew he would be in good hands.

And, while a camel segment had already been featured on the show, Larry's celebrity status earned him a segment on the show's roster as well. Just one of the advantages of being a celebrity!

On operation day, an unsuspecting Larry stood placidly in a wide-open pasture. He paid no attention to Jeff, the vet team, or the television crew. He just watched. On the sidelines, Jeff, too, watched and made the easy pronouncement to the camera, "I've neutered a camel before. I'm not afraid to spay/neuter any animal. The biggest challenge with neutering a camel is the anesthesia; getting him down and doing it safely."

With the anesthesia all set to go in the form of an injection, Hector had the job of administering the sedative. With a quiet but wary confidence, he walked up to Larry's unmoving figure and easily inserted the needle into the camel's left flank.

"He didn't even flinch!" said Jeff with a slight rise of his eyebrows. "We'll just wait for him to go down and then move on with surgery."

A few minutes later, as the anesthesia took effect, Larry began to sway

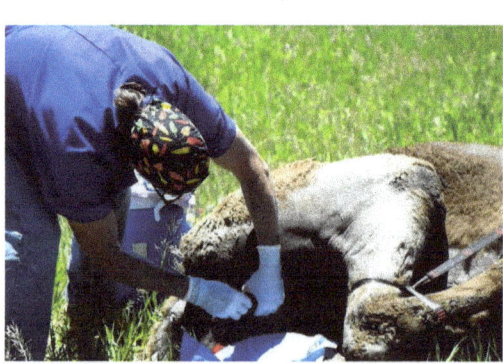

Dr. Jeff works on neutering Larry

and stagger. The team carefully helped guide him to the ground and within minutes the surgery was underway. This type of surgery, a specialty of Jeff's no matter what type of animal, proceeded easily with no complications.

"These are the biggest testicles I've ever taken off an animal!" exclaimed Jeff. "But I haven't done an elephant yet, though," he added with a grin. "I'm waiting for that one."

As the anesthesia wore off, Larry ambled back up with ease with only a little help needed from the team. "He'll be a new man in a few days," Jeff assured the Aurin family.

For the Aurins, the change was bittersweet. "Part of me is sad," said Mrs. Aurin, "because I was hoping we'd have camel calves here on the farm. But I am so much happier at the quality of Larry's life now after the surgery."

As for Larry, life goes on and he is back to his former easy-going self —still walking in the Fourth of July parades, still charming all his fans at various event appearances, and still just tolerating Camille.

Jeff and the Two Bears

The setting: The Wildlife Animal Sanctuary in Keenesburg, Colorado, a 1,300-acre, non-profit facility, housing over 500 exotic animals including lions, tigers, bears, wolves, and other rescued large carnivores.
The clients: Two bears – Lily, an Asiatic black bear who needs critical dental work – and Kelly, a Syrian brown bear who needs neutered.

Bear # 1 - Lily's Story

Once upon a time, Lily was a normal, good-looking bear. This was not true anymore and all those pictures spread on the computer screen proved the point. There she was, splayed uncharacteristically flat on her back, extremely obese, immobile, and almost comatose. Yes, that was what she looked like when rescued by the Wildlife Animal Sanctuary—a grotesque blob of an animal. Lily was the victim of a roadside zoo where wildlife was contained in an unnatural setting, treated poorly, and put on display for human enjoyment and profit.

"Lily is one of those classic rescue cases that came out of a horrible condition," sighed Jeff. "A roadside zoo kind of thing. She was kept in a small area, basically a small corn bin with concrete flooring, and her diet was predominantly wet dog food. She could never hibernate, never get away from people. I just don't understand how people don't realize that this is wrong."

"Since Lily arrived here," said Becca, the sanctuary's director, "she has lost 250 pounds. She still has more weight to lose. The ideal weight for

Lily's breed is between 100 to 150 pounds. She now eats very well and is on a proper diet for bears. She doesn't seem to have any issues in terms of pain. Her teeth, however, are not good and she needs dental work."

"In the wild, the bear's food is totally different," added Jeff. "They'll

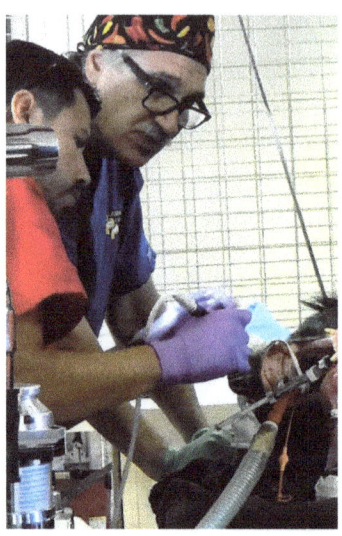

eat bugs and berries. The diet she was fed at this zoo explains a lot about her teeth and her obesity. The truth is, there is probably no other single thing that is more important in an animal's life than good dental health. And the fact is, if an animal has bad teeth, they have bad organs, and they don't live as long."

In the sanctuary's clinic, Jeff prepared the equipment to proceed with Lily's examination and dental procedure. A sedated Lily, still at least 100 pounds overweight, was raised up via a hydraulic lift unit and placed onto a large, square exam table. She was intubated and her mouth held open with

Hector performs dental work on Lily while Jeff observes

a special clamp to allow for access into her mouth and jaw area. Lily was also connected to a heart monitor which was necessary due to her weight.

"Any time you get heavy animals and they're on their side for an extended time, they can die from that," Jeff explained to Becca and his team. "All that fat is pushing on the diaphragm which is pushing on the heart and all the other organs, so we may have to ventilate her for a bit and monitor her heart rate as well."

Leaning over the edge of the exam table, Jeff peered closely into Lily's mouth, touching and tapping her teeth and jaw. "The back teeth are actually pretty good," Jeff noted, "but the front ones are all brown and covered with a thick film. They're not white."

As the sound of the dental drill whistled through the air, Jeff's everpresent right-hand man, Hector, who was doing the teeth cleaning and scaling procedure, remarked, "These are really small teeth. There's a lot of tartar; it's very thick and hard to get off. I'm trying to take off as much as possible as quickly as possible before the anesthesia wears off. Since every animal reacts differently to anesthesia, you're never sure exactly how much time you have."

Meanwhile, Jeff was keeping watch over the progress and monitoring Lily's vitals and heart rate. Shortly into the procedure, both Jeff and Becca noticed a significant drop in Lily's heart rate. Thinking quickly, Jeff said, "Let's see if rolling her over a little more will help. This is really dangerous, especially since she is having a hard time breathing."

Jeff called over his other vet tech, Ben, for assistance. "Ben, hop up on the exam table and hold up one of Lily's hind paws." Ben nimbly scrambled onto the exam table, pulled up Lily's paw, and propped it over his shoulder. Even with some of Lily's weight shifted from her side to her back, she still wasn't breathing well.

"We'll have to give her an injection of atropine which basically kicks up her heart rate," said Jeff emphatically. "That will make her breathe a little easier." And within moments after the injection, Lily's breathing and heart rate returned to normal.

Soon afterwards, Lily's dental procedure was complete, at least what could be done that day given the time under anesthesia. "There are some thoracic cavities that will have to wait for another visit," Jeff acknowledged. "But it's time to wake her up."

As Jeff takes one last look at Lily's teeth and mouth before she fully awakened, he gave his seal of approval and said with a grin to Hector, "Ah, minty fresh!" Moments later, Lily was then taken outside to her cage to recover from the anesthesia and Jeff moved on to work on the next bear.

Bear #2 - Kelly's Story

Kelly, on the brink of adulthood, was a bear who would never know the wild. He was born in captivity because his mother, pregnant with Kelly when she was rescued, was brought to the Wildlife Animal Sanctuary to live out the rest of her life.

Now that Kelly was two years old and maturing sexually, there was the real possibility that, should another Syrian female bear end up at the sanctuary, a mating could occur, resulting in one or more cubs. Since the sanctuary was not a breeding facility, it was time to circumvent that possibility by having Kelly neutered.

"I have actually worked with bears a little bit when I was a grad student," remembered Jeff. "Neutering a bear is pretty much like neutering a dog."

As Jeff made his first incision and proceeded with the surgery, halted only slightly as he cut through some tough skin layers, Hector stood by monitoring Kelly's heart. With a skilled hand and long-term experience working on wild animals, Jeff soon completed the surgery and both testicles were removed without complication.

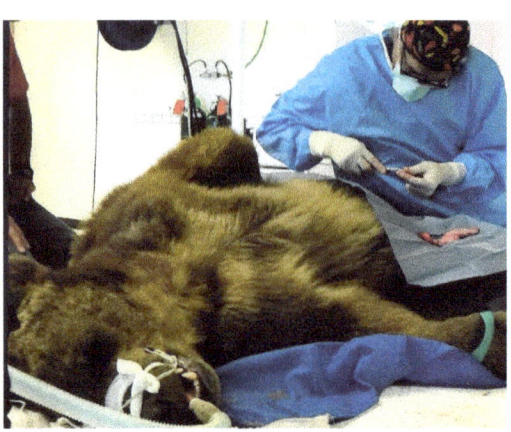

Jeff working on Kelly's neuter procedure

After the surgery, Jeff turned to Becca and reassuringly said, "Kelly's neuter was straightforward. I felt comfortable with it. There is a pretty small incision. I double tied everything so I don't think there will be a problem."

After an injection of antibiotics and anesthesia reversal medicine, Kelly was taken out to a recovery cage before being released back into the sanctuary. En route to the cage, Kelly emitted a low growl as the anesthesia began to wear off.

"We need to be careful and quick," warned Becca, as Kelly's growls began to increase in frequency and volume. "It's amazing how quickly bears can go from sleeping to not sleeping as they come out of anesthesia."

Almost as soon as Kelly was placed inside the cage, his eyes opened and his paws are began to swipe through the air. The team scurried to exit the cage.

"Every animal wakes up differently from anesthesia," commented Jeff as he watched Kelly awaken. "It's not so much a pain thing as it is a disorientation. Lots of animals make weird noises when they wake up. Once he really gets his consciousness back, he'll stop the erratic movements. He's probably disoriented right now. He just had his testicles cut, so he really just wants to go back home."

Thinking about the importance of working on these two bears and the Wildlife Animal Sanctuary, Jeff affirmed, "I've always worked with non-profits, and when I find a non-profit that I think is doing its job, I will help them out as I can. If I can go out and help those animals lead a normal, healthy life, why wouldn't I? That's what I got in the field to do."

A Tiger's Tale

Cucho, a male rescue tiger also living out his life at the Wildlife Animal Sanctuary in Keenesburg, Colorado, stood stock-still gazing at another tiger in the distance. A few pens over, watching him as well, was a new female tiger named Simba. Such began the daily "watch routine" that extended over several weeks as Cucho and Simba acknowledged each other from afar, following each other's movements and calling back and forth with roaring messages.

To sanctuary personnel, it not only seemed like love at first sight for the tigers, but also a desire for companionship; something missing from their life in captivity up until now and something the sanctuary was going to try and help facilitate.

"I just think it's going to be such an amazing and beautiful thing to see Cucho and Simba find the companionship they've never had before," mused Becca, the facility's director. "Since we are not a breeding facility, and these tigers can still mate, Cucho needs to be neutered before we can put them together. We will call Dr. Jeff to do the job. He has done a lot of work for us and knows what to do."

As Jeff arrived at the sanctuary, he recalled his previous work here and said, "This sanctuary is kind of the last stop for these animals and a place where they get to live out some really nice, normal, healthy lives. I've worked on Cucho before, and this time I'm back to neuter him. I've never neutered a tiger before; hopefully it won't be my last."

Awaiting Cucho's arrival to the on-site clinic, Jeff casually said to Hector and those standing nearby, "Neutering a tiger will be interesting.

They're just a big cat so everything is just going to be a lot bigger."

Hearing that remark, the others eyed him quizzically, and to his chagrin, Jeff suddenly realized both the gravity and enormity of the situation at hand. This was not just an oversized house cat he was operating on, but a large, wild animal that would hopefully stay fully anesthetized until he could complete his first-ever tiger neuter.

"No pressure here at all," murmured Jeff with bemusement.

Cucho finally arrived and his 300-pound body was hoisted up via a hydraulic lift onto the operating table. Even sedated, low growls rumbled forth from the tiger. Jeff held up one of Cucho's paws against his human hand in comparison and marveled at the size of the tiger's paw. Next, Cucho was intubated, mouth clamped open, and placed on a heart monitor as the procedure began. Time was of the essence.

From the first incision, Jeff was aware that this was really going to be a different kind of neuter. "Man, this skin is really thick," he grumbled with exasperation. "There's a lot of fat. It's really difficult. His skin is so tough. The scrotum is ridiculous."

Hector, once again serving as Jeff's assistant, watched closely, very concerned. "This has got to be one of the hardest neuters you've ever done, man."

"I really need to concentrate on this for a minute," Jeff said firmly. "Why don't you put a pair of gloves on, Hector? You can't believe how hard and fibrous this is. It's really tough."

After much effort, Jeff was finally able to cut off the first testicle and then the second one with a little more ease. He worked diligently to finish the procedure that took much longer than anticipated.

As he closed the incision site, he spoke to his team, and with obvious relief in his voice said, "That's good. I feel like everything is tied off. That was definitely not an easy neuter. It was the longest cat neuter in the world."

"I could tell that Jeff was sweating," recounted Hector. "I think that was the first time I ever had to glove in for a neuter with Jeff. It was a lot harder than he thought, but he did it."

With Cucho resting easily in the recovery pen after the surgery, Jeff stood outside the cage alongside Becca and Hector, watching as the tiger awakened, checking his movement and alertness.

"Cucho and Simba should be introduced to one another in about ten days," Jeff informed Becca, "after he recovers from the surgery. In the meantime, he'll be in this cage right next door to his girlfriend!"

"We're really hoping that the companionship between Cucho and Simba can help give them some quality of life," commented Becca. "Quality of life, and freedom to be as natural as possible, is a big part of what we do here at the sanctuary; to give them back the things that humans have taken away."

A Jaw-of-a-Problem for a Llama

For this out-of-clinic jaunt, Jeff and Dr. Nichols, his Planned Pethood colleague, headed to Salida, Colorado located high in the Rocky Mountains. Salida—population 5,400—is home to a 100-year-old ranching community with various livestock and backwoods services, including a working llama rescue herd. Since 1990, this llama herd has been hired out as pack animals by backwoods trekkers. It's a family owned and operated business that also gives back to the military community by providing special treks to veterans and their families, enabling them to get out in nature and be around animals.

"I grew up in a military family," Jeff informed Tom and Jennifer, owners of the llama herd. "My stepfather was in Vietnam for a year. We put our military personnel through a lot and I think that anyone who wants to reach out and help veterans is okay in my book."

The patient at this site was a one-year-old llama, Rhett, whose swollen jaw also had a protruding lump underneath the jaw bone. Haltering the llama, Jeff walked Rhett into the barn where he could be stabilized in a restraining chute for closer examination. Both doctors gently touched the protruding area to see if they could see or feel anything wrong.

"Could be an abscess," Jeff speculated. "Looks less likely to be a broken jaw. Let's get out the portable x-ray unit and take a look. It's important for us to find out what it is and if it's treatable."

With Rhett standing still in the chute, Dr. Nichols positioned the x-ray plate slightly behind Rhett's jaw. Jeff, holding up the imaging camera above his head and directing it towards the plate, quickly snapped the diagnostic x-ray.

Reviewing the x-ray with Dr. Nichols and Tom, Jeff said, "This area here on the x-ray is one big giant pocket. Something probably got stuck up there at one point. It looks perforated. I want to take a probe and open this pocket up, drain it, and inject it with antibiotics. Just by opening that up and flushing it out could potentially cure the problem."

In preparation for the procedure, a tarp was spread on the barn floor. After Dr. Nichols gave Rhett a sedative in his front leg, he was moved from the chute over to the tarp where he dropped easily to the ground. She then proceeded to shave the jaw and cheek areas to expose the area requiring treatment.

As Jeff tried to insert the probe into the lump, he found it difficult to get it past an incredibly hard jaw bone. "It's like trying to cut into concrete," exclaimed Jeff.

"I brought the drill," said Dr. Nichols. And utilizing that piece of equipment, the probe was able to be inserted into the lump.

"I'd like to flush that," Dr. Nichols asserted.

"Yes. Flushing is the key," agreed Jeff, "flushing, flushing, flushing to get out as much of the bacteria as we can. We'll use Betadine, an antiseptic that is also antimicrobial."

"I also want to inject penicillin into the jaw as well as a systemic antibiotic," said Dr. Nichols.

With the lump successfully drained and sutured, the jawline was now perfectly normal; draining indeed was the answer to the llama's jaw problem. Now Rhett needed to awaken from the anesthesia without hurting himself or someone else.

"You don't want a 350-pound animal bobbing up out of control after anesthesia," remarked Jeff. "You need to keep them calm so that when they do get their standing legs they won't get into trouble."

To help make this possible, the doctors first stretched out Rhett's legs and then folded them gently underneath his body which would enable him to get up easily. As Rhett awakened, he sat up and rested on his legs, but he was in no hurry to stand. To help coax him into a standing position, Jennifer rattled a can of food in front of him, just out of reach, and cooed, "You have to work for food this time."

In an instant, Rhett was up on his feet and eagerly ate the food proffered to him. "That hurt jaw certainly didn't stop him from eating!" chuckled Jeff.

As Jeff and Dr. Nichols prepared to depart, Jeff reached out and shook hands with Tom and Jennifer. "I'm really glad we could come up here today. Look at this beautiful Colorado day! The fact that you guys rescue these animals and work with veterans and their families, that means a lot to me."

As Jeff waved goodbye to Tom and Jennifer, Rhett was now back in his corral munching contentedly on some grass and gazing into the distance, oblivious to both Jeff's departure and the help he had received. But, that was okay in Jeff's book because Rhett, well once more, had only one priority now—more food!

The Case of the Limping Lion and A Matter of Pride

Orion, a male rescue lion, had a problem. He was noticeably limping and sometimes in pain. Most of the time, Orion ignored the pain and kept up the pace of running and pouncing alongside his fellow lions. He was, after all, the leader of the pride here at the Wildlife Animal Sanctuary.

Orion's plight did not go unnoticed, though, and it was not long before personnel at the sanctuary determined that the matter required veterinary attention. They promptly called in Jeff and his team to examine Orion, find out what the problem was, and see if it was treatable.

"This is my first time working with a lion," Jeff told the television crew filming this encounter for the *Dr. Jeff* show. "They're amazing animals. The lions on the premises here at the sanctuary were rescues out of Mexico, either from circuses or from people that tried to have them as pets.

"Today I'm looking at a male lion that's limping. It will take a few minutes to sedate him, then we'll get him over here into the van, and then to the on-site clinic. We'll have to work on him as fast as we can, before the anesthesia wears off."

Hector, who would be assisting Jeff on this visit, smiled a bit nervously as things were being set up in the clinic for Orion's exam.

"For me," recounted Hector, "this is round two of working on lions. I was scared and nervous that first time and I'm still a bit nervous this time, too. For Jeff, even though this is his first time with lions, he's not afraid. Jeff's not afraid of anything or any animal."

The van containing a sedated Orion arrived and it was now time to get to work. Orion, resting on a tarp, was hoisted with great effort out of the van by four men—Jeff, Hector, and two others—and placed on the exam room floor. "Whew!" grunted Jeff. "That is one big lion!"

Holding up one of Orion's paws against his own hand, Jeff murmured in awe, "Look at the size of that paw!"

"Yeah," agreed Hector, "with his claws out, this kitty would tear you up!"

"You can't conceive of the strength of these animals," stated Jeff. "Their muscle is different than ours; it's just sheer power, ten times stronger than our muscles!"

Proceeding with the examination, Jeff noted that Orion's leg must have been broken at some point. "The sanctuary personnel don't know how it happened," Jeff said to his staff. "Let's get some x-rays and see what the long-term prognosis is for that leg. If it's in the joint, they can take action now that will delay degenerative joint disease. If it isn't the joint, there's not a whole lot you can do about it. But, we can't make any decisions without information."

Using the portable x-ray machine, Jeff obtained an image of Orion's right hind leg. Looking at the x-ray with sanctuary director Becca, Jeff said, "Well, the joint itself looks pretty good. We just need another view of the knee itself."

To get a better view of the knee, while lifting and repositioning the hind leg, Jeff noticed a mass on the inside of Orion's leg just above his knee.

"Wait, something's wrong," he said. "What is that? Possibly a torn ACL. I don't see a break though. Let's x-ray that area."

Looking at the second x-ray image with Becca leaning over his shoulder, Jeff shook his head and said, "Man, this femur is curved and abnormally shaped. This bone over here is floating free and should not be here. This piece has been broken off and sealed back down to the tibia. Everything is abnormal on that knee. I don't know how this lion is walking on it. This is all bonded together; it's not supposed to be there and sticking out like it is."

As further explanation of his findings, Jeff leaned over the still sedated Orion, pulled up his leg with one hand and placed his other hand over the lump while moving the leg back and forth. "When I move this leg," Jeff demonstrated, "it doesn't extend the right way, and the knee area, this lump, it crunches really good. I just feel the crunching in my hand and it just looks totally abnormal."

"So what do we do?" asked Becca anxiously.

"Nothing," Jeff said candidly. "If he were a domestic cat, he would be a candidate for an amputation. He's not. You can't really have a three-legged wild cat around a bunch of other animals. It just doesn't work that way in the wild."

With the examination over and the sedation wearing off, the four-person team once again hoisted Orion back onto the van for transport back to the lion house for recovery. Soon, Orion was awake and alert, resting on his paws but not quite ready to get up.

"Orion is a feisty lion," Jeff noted to Becca and his staff. "He goes up to the other lions across the way and he's not afraid at all; he still uses that abnormal leg. I think the best way to treat this is with some of the newer drugs that have some real potent anti-inflammatories to help him manage the pain. Orion's going to get an anti-inflammatory in his food every day for the rest of his life."

Becca agreed. "We want to manage Orion so that he can stay as much of a lion as he possibly can, to help him be in a pride, be a king, and just really enjoy life."

"I think everything went really well," acknowledged Jeff as he and his team prepared to leave. "We got Orion sedated without too much trouble and we got him done pretty quick. Lions are amazing animals, they really are. And luckily," Jeff grinned, "they get fed really well here."

Mission Wolf

On this trek, the veterinary "pack" from Planned Pethood traveled to a remote area in the Sangre de Cristo mountain range near Westcliffe, Colorado. Their destination was a remote, 50-acre wolf sanctuary, situated high in the Rocky Mountains called Mission Wolf. As the facility came into view, the sound of howling wolves began to fill the air. They could sense that company was about to arrive.

"I came up here about 20 years ago and did eleven or so vasectomies on some wolves," Jeff told his team. "On this trip, we'll be working on wolf-hybrids. Hmm, this place is bigger now. They've added on."

Jeff's five-member pack was greeted warmly by facility owner Kent who smiled at Jeff and said, "I recognize that face!"

"It's been a while," replied Jeff as he and Kent shook hands. "It's good to see you."

By means of further introduction, Kent told the group some details about the facility. "Mission Wolf was formed in 1988 to take in the unwanted wolves, the 'pet' wolves, zoo wolves, movie wolves, those that can't go back to the wild. The shy ones who come here get a sanctuary; we hardly go near them. The outgoing ones get a purpose, to teach compassion to the people who visit this sanctuary."

"Our patient today, Talon," continued Kent, "is more dog than wolf but he has enough wolf to make him a little wild. He's not eating. We haven't been able to look in his mouth. I don't know what's going on."

"Let's go visit the wolves," said Jeff.

"What's the game plan?" Hector asked.

"The game plan is not to get bit!" teased Jeff.

In actuality, the game plan involved protocol particular to wolves. Before Jeff could examine the patient, he and the team had to meet and be accepted by the rest of the wolf pack. It's what one might call the "wolf thing" to do.

As they all walked up to the fence enclosure, Kent instructed them accordingly. "I want you guys to walk in with intent. Don't even look at the

120

wolves. Look straight ahead."

Meanwhile, Kent calmly opened the enclosure gate and continued his instructions saying, "Come right on through. These are wolf-dogs and you can see they are more outgoing with us. But don't be fooled. These are wild animals. Let's sit down over here and see if they will say hi to us."

Arranging themselves in a semi-circle formation, some sitting on a log and some on the ground, the Planned Pethood pack waited to see if they would be approached by members of the wolf pack and gain acceptance.

"The biggest problem," Jeff told his team, "is that people see wolves and they think they're 'cool' and want them as pets. Then they do wolf-dog crosses or wolf-hybrids and these animals just don't make good pets; their behavior is definitely different. They're not dogs and because of that, literally thousands of these wolf-dogs and wolf-hybrids are euthanized every year because people can't handle them."

As the humans sat, waiting for the wolves to come to them, each person was, in turn, greeted by one of the wolves with licks to their faces and mouths. The humans resisted the temptation to wiggle, squirm, or push the wolves away as they accepted the wolf greeting.

"What they're trying to do," explained Kent, "is get next to your teeth. Once they get their teeth against yours, they will usually back off. It's a symbol of respect. They want to show you that they're not a threat to you. The wolves are telling us that we're dominant. It's like a greeting ceremony."

"Yes," Jeff agreed. "They're just checking you out. That's what they do."

Now that the wolf pack had accepted the human pack, they could proceed to meet and greet Talon, the alpha male of the group, who was being held in a separate enclosure.

"We brought Talon out to this enclosure," said sanctuary co-owner, Mike, "separating him from his mate so he could be examined and treated."

"Talon is probably in a lot of pain," Jeff noted in response, "so if we can get him back to eating normal, that's what we're going to do. We'll have to inject him with a sedative and hope nobody gets bit. We have no idea what we're walking into. All we know is we won't be able to look into his mouth until we get him under."

Upon entering this enclosure, as they did with the other wolves, the humans sat down and waited for Talon to approach them. They already had the benefit of carrying the wolf pack's scent, so it wasn't long before Talon became accustomed to these new humans in his midst.

"Are you comfortable holding his head?" Jeff asked Mike as he rested a reassuring hand on Talon's backside. "Yes," Mike replied, wrapping his arms around Talon's neck. At the same time, Hector approached slowly from behind, sedative-filled syringe in hand, and injected Talon in his upper hind leg at which Talon yelped and jumped back despite Mike's embrace.

"Sorry buddy. I know that stung a little." Mike said to Talon in a soothing voice.

The sedative soon took effect and Talon dropped to the ground. He was then carried to a small clinic room nearby for the examination. As Jeff opened his jaw and peered into Talon's mouth he said, "It's not looking good for the home team. These teeth are terrible. The front lower canines are just broken and rotting or loose. Does he like to chew a lot?" Jeff asked Mike.

"He loves to chew!" Mike acknowledged. "He'll usually get some ribs and chews on those."

"Some animals are really good at chewing," Jeff replied, "and a little bit of chewing is great, but a whole lot of chewing on really hard things can crack teeth."

To help Talon with his mouth problem, Jeff removed one of the lower canine teeth, along with three of the worst teeth in his mouth. Holding up the removed canine tooth, Jeff explained, "This tooth was probably causing the most pain. It was decayed below the gum line and almost totally worn and broken off on top. Hopefully this will help solve the problem. We'll see how he does having these teeth removed." Jeff then instructed Mike not to give Talon any bones for at least five days.

"Talon needs to wake up and then we'll do a round of antibiotics," Jeff told his staff. "The mouth heals really fast. In three to five days the mouth will be totally different. I suspect Talon will be back to eating normally pretty quickly."

Turning to Mike, Jeff queried, "The last time I was here, we didn't put the treated wolves back in with the other wolves until they were 100% awake. Talon is just in with his mate, right?"

"His stepdaughter is in there too," Mike informed Jeff. "Since Talon is the alpha of that group, we have to make sure he's 100% awake and alert or she will try to challenge him and he won't be able to fight back. If he's doing all right, we'll put him back in with those two this evening. If he needs extra time, we'll wait until tomorrow."

The job completed, and Talon awake from his sedation and on the mend, Jeff and the team made their way to the van for the trip home. Jeff and Hector, the last to exit the sanctuary, stood on the porch of the main office cabin and looked out over the landscape. In that moment, a rolling wave of wolf howls began to fill the air. Listening for a moment, Jeff then tilted his head upward and pealed off several of his own wolf howls in response—a goodbye to all stating that, "Dr. Jeff was here."

"I think you are part wolf, Jeff!" asserted Hector with a grin on his face as he watched Jeff howling. "What are they saying back to you?"

"They're saying that they like *Dr. Jeff Rocky Mountain Vet*!" Jeff smiled.

As the human pack departed, driving into the sunset and making the trek back to Denver, echoes of wolf howls lingered on the wind and in their minds. It was another successful trek, another animal helped, and an adventure that will long be remembered by one and all.

Jeff and the Jaguar - A Most Memorable Tale

It was 2019, and Jeff and the TV crew were visiting the Planned Pethood International Training Center in Merida, Mexico as part of Jeff's ongoing mission to work with new veterinarians and students.

"Planned Pethood Mexico is open, growing, and thriving," explained Jeff. "The fact is that we also want to expand what we do here even more. So on this trip, we're reaching out to local animal and welfare groups who don't have access to adequate veterinary care. Today I'm going out to the

Vallazoo and Animal Sanctuary in Valladolid, Mexico as they recently lost their veterinarian."

Elaborating, Jeff continued, "There's a seven-year-old jaguar named Lola there that needs spayed. Lola came from another zoo and has had pregnancy issues in the past. Since she'll be living here with an intact male jaguar, there is a concern for her health if she got pregnant again. The reality is, spay/neuter works for wildlife just like with domestic animals. If we can make Lola feel better and live a little longer, then why not?"

Arriving at the sanctuary, Jeff and the sanctuary's animal control officer walked over to the enclosure where Lola was pacing rapidly back and forth. She emitted a series a series of piercing, raspy growls while eyeing the men with unveiled ferocity, ready to pounce at the slightest provocation. "She's looking at me like I'm breakfast," Jeff murmured aloud to the officer.

Safe on the other side of the fenced enclosure, Jeff and the animal control officer watched Lola intently as well. Lola needed to be sedated for the spay surgery to be performed, but hitting a moving target is no easy task. The officer positioned his dart gun, loaded with sedation medication, through an opening in the fence, got set, aimed, and then waited. His aim and timing needed to be perfect in order for the dart to hit its target, Lola's shoulder, and for the sedation to have maximum effectiveness.

Several minutes went by and then...pfft! The dart whizzed through the air and reached its target. Although Lola went down immediately, the nearby four-man assistance team waited a few more minutes to assure that she was completely out before entering the enclosure. The race was now on and time was of the essence.

With concerted effort, the team lifted the 130-pound jaguar onto a canvas stretcher, carried her several hundred feet to the vehicle and hoisted her up onto the bed of a pickup truck. Traveling over rough terrain for several minutes, they transported Lola to the on-site infirmary, a small, one-room adobe structure with basic minimal equipment.

Lola was brought into the building and placed on the operating table. Suddenly, there were a dozen people cramming into the small room to watch this operation: the *Dr. Jeff* film crew, curious staff members and onlookers from the Valla facility, plus Jeff and his assistant.

The number of people present didn't bother Jeff in the least. His main concern was only how much time he had before Lola's sedation wore off because there was still a lot to do: prepping the surgery site, setting up the oxygen and monitoring systems along with mouth and teeth guards, the surgery itself, and then getting Lola back to the enclosure for recovery before the anesthesia wore off.

With things moving rapidly along in good order, Jeff took a momentary pause before beginning the surgery to take a close-up look at the magnificent animal in front of him.

"Look at that coat," he marveled as his hand stroked the animal's fur. Then, holding one of Lola's paws up against his own hand, examining the contrast in size and contour, Jeff continued to express his awe about this large, wild animal before him and exclaimed, "That's a pretty big paw and she has some *real* claws. What an amazing animal!"

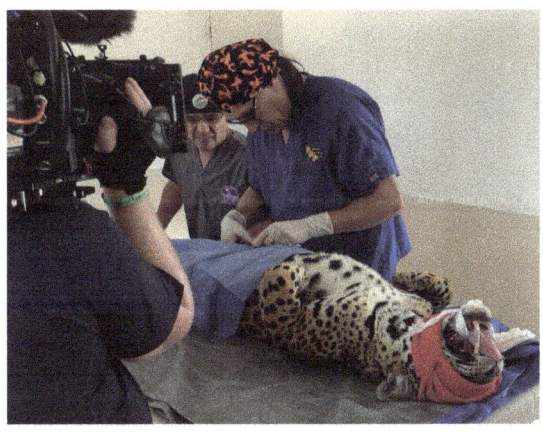

Jeff blocks out every distraction to focus on the surgery at hand as the TV camera rolls

Time for the surgery. Focusing strictly on the task at hand, Jeff worked to make the necessary incision by first cutting through an extremely tough hide, then a thick skin layer, and finally a layer of muscle. Sweat trickled on his forehead. Finally, after several long moments of struggling, the area was opened sufficiently to remove the reproductive organs and tie off the vasculature.

Now to close the surgery site. As he once again tackled the thick layers of muscle and skin, Jeff wondered how much time was left of Lola's sedation. He was keenly aware that Lola could wake up at any moment. Working with calm quickness and efficiency, Jeff finally managed to close the incision site. His last task before sending Lola off to recover from the surgery was administering an injection of pain medication and an antibiotic that would aid in post-surgical recovery and healing.

With everything now completed, Lola was again hoisted onto the bed of the pickup truck and hurriedly transported back to her enclosure pen for recovery. Just in time, too, because no sooner did Jeff close the enclosure gate, than Lola began to recover from the anesthesia, emitting a rolling series of loud growls and rumbles.

"She's growling and that's good," Jeff smiled. "If I heard that sound out in the wild, I'd be scared!"

Catching his breath at the end of the day and mulling over what he has since claimed as one of his most memorable experiences, Jeff grinned and made a telling statement about his veterinary life. "Lions, tigers, bears, and now jaguars," he said. "It's really cool to be able to do something like this and to help wild animals. It's certainly not one of those things you think about when you're in vet school!"

CHAPTER 9
THE GRRR FACTOR AND OTHER PEOPLE TALES

Dr. Jeff's work and life is a nexus between that of helping animals and helping people. The simple fact is that, for Jeff, animals and people are interconnected, and the philosophy that describes his life might be summed up with this equation:

(Animals + People) x Connections = Life

In addition to the animal tales that contribute to Jeff's life and practice —the first part of the equation—there are also tales from the people without whom the story would be incomplete.

A Partner's Tale

When Jeff starts talking about Dr. Petra Mickova, DVM, he can talk for a long time. "Petra is brilliant!" Jeff constantly affirms. Married to Jeff since 2014, Petra is also his partner in the practice and holds in her heart the same passion for providing care and service to animals and the people who love them.

Given the age difference between Jeff and Petra, and the fact that they literally lived in separate worlds before they met, such a match might never have occurred had it not been for Jeff's international work, outreach, and training efforts. It all started via the Planned Pethood clinic in Bratislava, Slovakia.

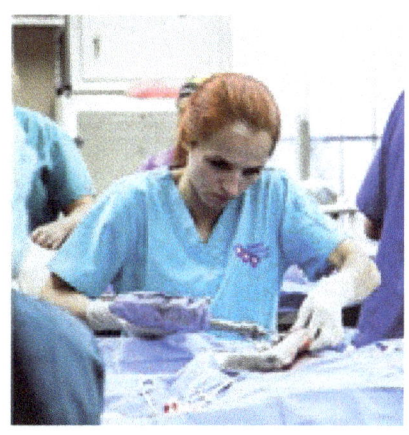
Petra performing a surgery

"I worked at the clinic in Slovakia with Dr. Hudec years before I met Jeff," explained Petra. "Years later, when I was in vet school in the Czech Republic, I saw and recognized Jeff and said, 'Oh, you're the guy I used to work for in Slovakia.'

So Jeff invited me to the United States to do an internship, like he always does for everybody, and I came."

And then she stayed. The relationship blossomed and a marriage resulted that made for a powerhouse team, both professionally and personally.

Interestingly, where the *Dr. Jeff* show was concerned, their union was not made evident during the first season. "Although we were mar-

ried quite a bit before Season 1," remembered Petra, "I didn't officially 'exist' yet as a partner or his wife; I wasn't mentioned in any of the episodes during Season 1. The way it appeared on the show, we got married between Seasons 1 and 2. I guess they finally realized they had to bring me into the show 'officially' since everyone kept asking about 'that redhead in the background who assisted Jeff with so many surgeries!'"

When thinking about Jeff and the effect he has had on her life, what Petra likes best about him is how they complement one another.

Jeff and Petra

"Jeff is just a really good human being," Petra said. "He's fascinating and has a complicated personality with many layers. For me, he's just the right combination of the 'tough guy' type who is, at the same time, really sweet. We clicked very quickly and on a very deep level. I think it's fascinating that we connected and fell in love despite being very different in terms of age, where we lived, and who we are as individuals. We could not be more different but we are very much in love."

Petra continued, "The one thing that I find fascinating about Jeff, over and over again, is that even though we've been together for a long time, he truly thinks outside of the box like nobody I've ever seen. He thinks bigger than anybody else."

Reflecting further, Petra commented, "He is, as Esther Mechler has said, one of

Petra with their dog, Fred

those people who is larger than life, especially with his veterinary work. And he can actually pull it off at the end, which is the fascinating part. He has so many different parts to his personality. And, most of all, we are committed to the same legacy for Planned Pethood."

Tales from Colleagues

Working with Jeff as a colleague has influenced many veterinarians over the years on a variety of levels. Here are tales from two vets who, inspired by Jeff and having worked at Planned Pethood, have followed their passion for animal care.

Dr. Lauren Makowski, DVM

"I was so lucky to have been there," exclaimed Dr. Lauren Makowski reflecting on her time at Planned Pethood. "A lot of people in this area of Colorado know about Dr. Jeff's place and when I told them I was going to work there, they were like, 'Good for you! That's amazing!'"

Dr. Lauren remembered her first weeks at Planned Pethood and said, "When I started working there, I was a little intimidated at first. Intimidated by the case load, the number of surgeries, and the chances they give to pets that don't have a chance at other places. It is a very unique practice. They get a lot of crazy cases, but that's exactly why I wanted to be there. Just to keep learning!"

Dr. Lauren continued, "When I got called in to do my interview, I think it was Hector who called me, he said, 'Come on in and we will set you up to talk with Dr. Young.' I didn't put the two things together that Dr. Young was Dr. Jeff, even having watched the show. So when we met and I realized the connection, I was so astonished because I was meeting someone that I really looked up to—my idol! Now I feel like we're friends. He's a really great mentor, and that was a life-changing job for me."

Dr. Joel Stone, DVM

"As a veterinarian who has worked in the field for almost 30 years, working on large and small animals, I wanted to be somewhere where I felt like I could help people with their animals and do it at a reasonable price," stated Dr. Joel Stone.

"In a lot of companies—and I did work for the VCA (Veterinary Corporation of America)—the pricing, from my perspective, was getting ridiculous. Working at Planned Pethood was an opportunity for me to do a lot of good medicine and learn a lot of surgery. Jeff is an amazing surgeon, and Petra is a brilliant woman, and they're both fun to work with."

Dr. Joel continued, "I think Jeff has a very realistic view of veterinary medicine. He wants to help. I think his underlying thinking is that he's in veterinary medicine not for the money, not even for the animals in some ways, but it's kind of between him and God, and he wants to do what is right. I think that changes your perspective of how you work and the level of energy you give; it's different, and because of that, the work to help animals becomes your all."

He added, "I've adopted that viewpoint as well, and it's made my personal life in veterinary medicine so much better. It's between me and God and I know what God wants me to do, so I'm going to do it. That's just a little twist of thinking that for me has made a huge difference."

The GRRR Factor and a Samurai Friend

It all started with a cat that needed a little bit of veterinary care.

The cat's owner, James Bedwell, a dojo and martial arts instructor and a personal trainer at Steel 29 Fitness in Denver, brought his cat to Jeff via a referral from Janet Hattlestad, Jeff's second wife.

It was a straightforward case of veterinary care and service that might have ended after those first few visits were it not for the conversations that started up between Jeff and James.

"After the vet visits, I started talking to James about the programs he offered and his background," remembered Jeff. "I was very interested in adding to my fitness program, especially when I saw how Janet had benefitted from her personal training with James and his programs. We hit it off right away. There was a connection and camaraderie between us that grew into mutual respect and regard."

"Jeff wanted to regain his fitness after having a double lateral knee surgery and a 40% lung removal surgery on his left side following his first bout with cancer," recalled James.

"While doing personal training, Jeff also took up the Japanese martial art of dojo with me. This regimen involves a way of life—a journey into ancient traditions and mastery of martial arts training that focuses not only on physical techniques but also on mental and spiritual development similar to the samurai code of ethics."

Over the next several years, Jeff worked out with James at Steel 29 Fitness in the early mornings at least five days a week before going into the

clinic. Even though Jeff was busy with his practice, the television show, running and coaching, and a second round of cancer treatments that sometimes wore him out, the workouts continued with both Jeff and James rallying and calling upon an essence of energy and inner strength.

James Bedwell of
Steel 29 Fitness

"We've got that GRRR factor," Jeff told James one day. "It's what I see in all those animals that survive when everything says they shouldn't. They have this GRRR factor in them and they *want* to live. Having that factor present can make all the difference between living and dying for an animal."

James agreed wholeheartedly and together they adopted the GRRR factor into their own training and mental mindset.

"When you come to be a part of the dojo training," explained James, "your attitude must be one of discipline, courage, acts of righteousness, and good moral behavior. It's a dance with the samurai mentality. It involves physical health and a mental attitude of living every day to the fullest. There is no doubt that Jeff has that GRRR factor in him."

James continued, "One of the most memorable moments I had with Jeff was during his second bout with cancer. During that time, we trained harder than ever. I pushed him through the pain to another level. Because of the drugs Jeff was on, he sometimes got sick during training, but he never stopped. He continued training."

James added, "There was, and is, an unspoken bond between us of life, death, honor, integrity, and strength. It's what keeps us alive. It's what tribe and community are—our energy with one another. It's that GRRR factor and I'm proud of and inspired by my association with Jeff."

"Dear Dr. Jeff et al."
Tales from Student Interns

Dr. Jeff is passionate not only about animals and animal care, but equally as passionate about passing that knowledge on and training new veterinarians. Always on the lookout for prospective students and willing to provide for their training, Jeff continues to develop his Planned Pet-hood International Training Center and offers veterinary internships, at no cost to the students, along with free room and board. These internships provide much-needed opportunities for both hands-on experience and the challenge of applying book learning to a real-life setting.

Upon departing from the learning experience, the students often write letters and notes to Jeff in appreciation—a bird's eye view as it were—of how the pupil has been inspired and helped by their teacher.

Here, in their own words, are a handful of those views that make up the "nest" of education provided by Jeff, Petra, and the team at Planned Pethood International.

~ From Student Interns Diarra Oliveira and Francisco Batalha ~
Dear Planned Pethood Family,

We spent one month at the Planned Pethood Hospital and it was one of the best experiences we ever had. Coming not only to a different country, but also to a different continent, at first felt a little scary, but all our fears went away once we set foot in the hospital and everyone was so friendly and welcoming.

Here we were able to practice surgeries with the vets, and medical skills with the technicians. We couldn't have had a better experience. We are very grateful for our time and we are definitely going to miss every-body.

We want to thank especially Dr. Jeff Young for this opportunity, as well everyone at Planned Pethood who were so incredible with us.

~ *From Student Intern Sarah Rollins* ~

Dear PPI Team,

Working together with you all over the past three weeks has been eye opening and one of the most fun externship experiences I've had in vet school.

Learning in an environment that is open, full of laughs and good times is an amazing experience.

Everyone on the PPI team has been so welcoming and fun to work with! Although I originally scheduled my externship to gain more surgical skills and confidence, I am excited to have walked away with so much more.

Dr. Jeff, thank you for reminding me what veterinary medicine is all about and why we get into this line of work.

It is hard to keep things in perspective while in school, being blackmailed by the overwhelming amount of debt and stresses of starting off a career.

Seeing firsthand how much good can come from vets that care has reminded me that money comes and goes. Debt will always be around, but the differences in the animal and owners lives we can make—that is long-standing and life changing!

The clinic and atmosphere you have created is one-of-a-kind and is focused on the animals more than the bottom line.

The perspective of practicing good medicine at a reasonable and affordable price is something that will stick with me long into my career.

Seeing that it is possible firsthand proves that the veterinary field can change for the better.

Thank you for pushing me to try new things, techniques, and to get my hands dirty.

You have been an amazing mentor and I appreciate you taking the time to answer all of my questions and correcting so many misconceptions!

You have instilled a confidence and drive in me that I can do any surgery I choose—so long as I have great surgical skills and the desire to always learn.

Thank you so much for welcoming me to Colorado with open arms!

~ *From Student Intern Chris Edwards* ~

Jeff,

When I started in vet medicine, I had a close mentor, Dr. Brown, that grew my interest in surgery. He taught me realistic, common-sense medicine and was always willing to teach. He retired two years after we started working together and it crushed me. I thought I'd never find another mentor that truly wants me to learn and grow.

Quickly after meeting you and Petra, I found myself to be the luckiest student ever. What are the odds of me finding mentors that care about me as much as Dr. Brown? Pretty slim, so I know I was truly blessed to have the opportunity to work and have fun with you all.

You and Petra have taught me so much in the hospital that I am way ahead of my friends—only because of y'all. Beyond knowledge and hands-on skills, you two have grown my confidence and overall mindset. I love learning and think of myself as a motivated individual.

The drive that you and Petra have to constantly learn and improve is infectious and has shown me a level of motivation beyond what I already have. I cannot wait to see my knowledge grow even faster with this high bar y'all have set for personal accountability and expansion of knowledge and interests. I love working with y'all so much. I couldn't get the smile off my face when I finally arrived.

I cannot put into words how thankful and appreciative I am for all the cool things you showed me and the places you've taken me to. I've fallen in love with Colorado and know there is no other place I want to call home.

When I'm with y'all, I always say, "I had the best day ever today," and then you take me somewhere even cooler then that's *the best day ever. I've had many of these "best days ever" with you two.*

Some of these best days include going to the cabin with y'all and Petra and finding a moose antler (that's the centerpiece of my room now).

...Teching for you for the first time when you yelled for someone to get you a surgery pack and I was the only one in the room and you ended up double tabling surgeries that day—it was too cool.

...Or the "best day" when we hiked Leadville for the first time...and then the second hike.

Yesterday topped all those days, though, when you and I were ligating splenic vessels together—something I'll never forget. You just looked at me and said, "Do it!" and I did.

I can't wait to keep coming back and I can't wait for the day I am a licensed DVM at PPI. I also can't wait to see the many adventures and surgeries we will get ourselves into in the future. I appreciate you two more than you could ever imagine.

~ *From Student Intern Amanda Topolski* ~

Dear Planned Pethood International Team,

I am not sure how to express what this experience meant to me in words, but I am going to try.

My mom got me into watching Dr. Jeff Rocky Mountain Vet *years ago and, since then, it has been a dream of mine to experience working here at PPI. Well, the reality of this experience has been even better than I ever dreamed.*

Since day one, everyone here has been nothing but welcoming, kind, and supportive. Your patience while I have learned has helped improve my confidence so much, from jugular blood draws to surgical skills (I have done over 80 solo surgeries during my month here, which seems crazy to say).

And, having the opportunity to scrub in and assist Dr. Jeff and Dr. Petra in surgeries is something I will never forget (screwing a pin into a bone? Suturing intestines? Amazing.)

This experience has been more than just technical—you have been such amazing mentors, teaching me to not be afraid, to always strive to keep learning, and to trust in myself and my abilities.

I am going to take what I learned here—the technical skills, the mindset, and the confidence — as I continue my journey to becoming a veterinarian.

I hope to have the opportunity to work with each and every one of you again in the future (and, if you're looking for a new grad vet at your new place, I'm your girl).

Thank you all again from the bottom of my heart.

Melinda Grohol

~ From Student Intern Meje Bogetej ~

Dear All,

Let me say a big thank you for your great hospitality and warm welcome. The last three weeks have been amazing, not only for all the new things that I have learned, but also for all the new people that I have met.

I have been waiting for my visit to PPI for quite a long time and in the end, it turned out to be much better than I would ever expected. I know how hard it is nowadays to find somebody that would share the knowledge and skills with you and that is why I am extremely grateful for an opportunity like this.

A special thank you goes to Dr. Jeff and Dr. Petra. It makes me really happy that there are still vets and people like you out there. Thank you for your dedication and thank you for everything you are doing for your patients. I admire your work and I truly believe this world would be a better place for the animals if there would be more people like you. I wish you all the best with your new training center and all your future plans.

I hope I can come to visit you again and you are always very welcome if you ever want to come in Slovenia. I thank you for everything.

~ From Student Intern Jessica Marsh ~

Dear Everybody at Planned Pethood,

Thank you so much for allowing me the opportunity to do my preclinical membership with you. I've enjoyed working with you again.

Thank you for taking the time to teach me and work with me on my skills. Everyone here is nice and I always enjoy seeing the side of you they don't show on TV.

I hope to be able to volunteer this summer and to be able to do an externship with you in my fourth year. Thank you for all you have done for me. I hope to work with you again soon.

~ From Student Intern Jessica Sims ~

Dear Dr. Jeff,

Had an awesome time volunteering on my internship with you guys! Thank you for taking the time to teach Katie [fellow student intern] and me and for giving us so much hands-on experience! I feel a lot more confident in my orthopedic surgery knowledge and can't wait to come back after graduation to learn more. The whole team was awesome!

Thanks everyone!

~ *From Student Intern Katie Siegfried* ~

Dear Dr. Jeff,

This two-week internship was an incredible experience! Thank you to everyone for teaching us and making us feel like one of the family.

I'm so grateful for all the hands-on experience and the ability to scrub in on so many surgeries. I have learned so many skills that I will use in my career.

Thanks to all the amazing techs and staff for showing us the ropes.

And a special thank you to all the veterinarians that made this possible.

Hope to visit you again soon!

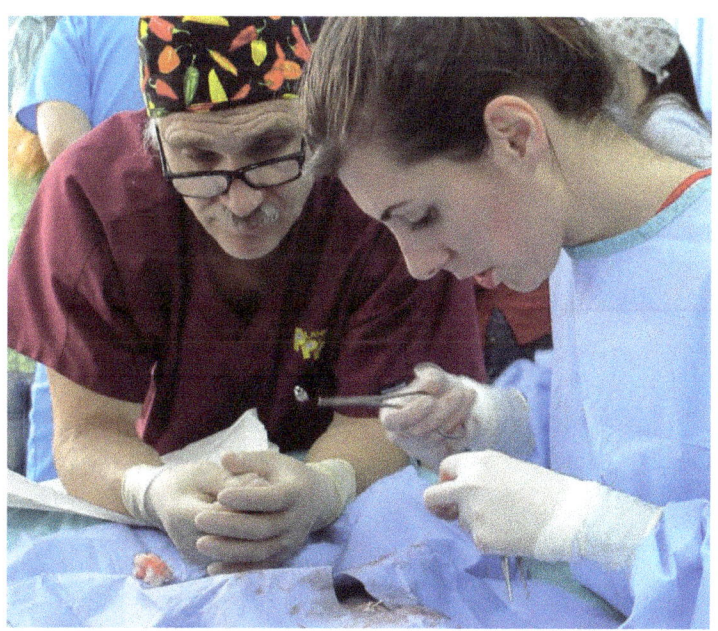

Jeff in teaching mode with an intern

CHAPTER 10
THE LEGACY

Relocating to Conifer, Colorado in May of 2023 after decades in Denver, and still in the wake of post-COVID recovery, was a risky move for Dr. Jeff and the practice, now a 100% nonprofit named Planned Pethood International (PPI).

While the move fulfilled Jeff's long-held dream of living and working in the mountains rather than the city, there remained the daunting task of rebuilding the practice in a new community while also providing for Dr. Petra's future and the legacy of Planned Pethood.

"My goal," said Jeff, "is to leave PPI in a position that it will flourish long after I'm gone." And true to form, Jeff proceeded forward, always in motion, following his one-word mantra—"Onward!"

While it had been some time since Jeff was the "new kid on the block" with his veterinary practice, he knew from experience exactly what it would take to become known, established, and settled in this present community—local involvement.

So he set to work on an ongoing series of events that quickly earned him a foothold in the area and helped to secure Planned Pethood a place in the community.

It started, and continues, with his tried-and-true low-cost spay/neuter clinics. Added to the mix is participation in community events, fundraising dinners, radio talk show segments, public service announcements about pets, and revitalizing the long-standing Intermountain Humane shelter. Along the way, new veterinary and administrative staff were also hired to accommodate the ongoing expansion of services. With all of this, Planned Pethood is once again weaving its reputation and legacy into the hearts of animal lovers all around, this time from the Conifer mountain community and beyond.

Featured and captioned on the following page are promotional materials representing a few highlights from PPI's participation in the Conifer community over the past few years.

Left: Poster for a low cost vaccine clinic
Above: a dog in line at a vaccine clinic
expectantly awaits his turn

Left: PPI staff participate in the
Conifer Christmas parade

Bottom left: Poster from an
Intermountain Humane community
event, Dogtoberfest!

Bottom right: Publicity poster of
pet care info broadcast on KOSI,
a Denver radio station

In the trail of all this local involvement and activity, two other events occurred that further underscored the impact of both PPI and Intermountain Humane in the Conifer region.

One of those events happened in April 2024 when Intermountain Humane (IMH) was awarded the 2024 Non-Profit of the Year Award by the Conifer Area Chamber of Commerce. This notable award served to acknowledge both the long-standing work of IMH and celebrate its ongoing renaissance as part of Planned Pethood.

Left: The award statuette
Right: IMH staffers
Nancy Parks,
Susan Rieger, Jeff,
and Roxy Buzas
at the award ceremony

Another memorable event was the gift of a unique, hand-carved wooden "welcome" sign for PPI, presented to Jeff by renowned Conifer artist and woodcarver, Dennie Ibbotson, as a thank you to Jeff and the PPI team for saving his dog's life. Dennie devoted over 300 hours of his time to create the sign that is now displayed in the entryway lobby at PPI. A sign of welcome, it is also a symbol of mutual respect, talent, kindness, and generosity between two humans united by the mutual care for an animal in need.

Artist Dennie Ibbotson unveiling the sign he carved for PPI

With each passing month, Jeff and Petra continue to develop Planned Pethood as a tour de force in veterinary care and services to plant roots in the mountain community. In addition to ongoing local activities and programs, multiple other projects are in progress, including the redevelopment and relocation of Intermountain Humane to the PPI campus that will integrate clinic services with an animal shelter.

"I've always believed," said Jeff, "that animal shelters should do more

The new PPI/IMH logo

that just house animals; they should be able to treat those animals, too. That's why I think every humane society should have a full-service veterinary hospital. This is why we're combining Intermountain Humane with Planned Pethood International—to create a new shelter, smaller [than the original Intermountain Humane] on purpose, but better for the animals.

Our focus will be on the cases that need us most: the sick, the injured, the ones other shelters might turn away."

Describing some of the special features of the new shelter, Jeff continued, "We're going to have heated indoor/outdoor dog runs, an incredible state-of-the-art cattery on one level which will be the real 'cat's pajamas' that's for sure! The cattery will have bigger cages, much more sunlight, and will be a good distance away from where the dogs are because barking dogs can be very stressful on cats."

This new shelter, like all PPI efforts, reflects Jeff's intense passion for animals—how they're treated and cared for. "I've been doing this for decades," said Jeff, "patching up street dogs, dodging feral cats, and helping the animals no one else wants to deal with. And I've seen those animals come back to life. That's what animals do—they trust and they forgive. They give us humans their all, even when they've been given nothing in return. And that's why we're building a new shelter that's different. A shelter that's not just full of cages and concrete, but a real space for healing, hope, and second chances."

Onward!

The word around Planned Pethood these days is, as always, onward! And contrary to numerous false posts on social media about his imminent or permanent demise, Jeff exclaimed, "I'm not dead yet! I don't plan on retiring. I'll die with my boots on, doing what I love best, working with animals."

Reflecting upon other possible endeavors for the future, Jeff remarked, "I really want to travel a bit more. I want to go to places like Egypt and India to work with and educate veterinarians in those areas. While there's a lot of good work with animals going on all over the world, it comes down to the fact that there are only a handful of us out there teaching. We must teach more veterinarians to do basic care for animals like spay/neuter, dental work, abscesses, and treating fleas and ticks. It's great to have high-end specialists, but most animals simply need the basics."

From all of his work and experience in the veterinary field, Jeff knows that education, along with hands-on training, is the most effective way to help new veterinarians and keep programs moving forward.

"The truth is," elaborated Jeff, "you can be a really good spay/neuter surgeon anywhere in the world, but those efforts will be lost if you're the only person doing it. If, however, you teach ten other veterinarians to do spay/neuter, then suddenly you have an army to help address the problem of animal overpopulation."

Which is exactly what happened in Mexico. "Through PPI Mexico and Dr. Tony," stated Jeff, "we've created hundreds of spay/neuter surgeons. When we do a spay/neuter clinic now in Mexico, we make a few phone calls and we have vets lining up to volunteer. We now have the ability to impact cities or small towns struggling with animal overpopulation because of the number of trained vets we have on hand; vets who can perform spay/neuter surgeries on two, three, four, or even 500 animals in a day—that's crazy when you think about it! There have never been mega clinics like this anywhere in the world, along with training programs, until we started doing them."

It all goes to show the PPI philosophy of "think globally, act locally" in action. Starting locally, each service builds upon the next, and the next. It all adds up along the way, combining into a cascade of service that ultimately spans the globe.

"I really believe," said Jeff, "that if you give to your community, they will give back to you. It's okay to make a living as a veterinarian, and it's okay to give back, too, with programming and training."

For Jeff, a veterinarian constantly going beyond the boundaries to help animals, the bottom line is that animals are an integral part of our human lives, whether as companions, pets, or as creatures we can admire and from whom we can learn. As such, animals deserve the care and respect of humans to help strengthen and maintain the invaluable human/animal bond that connects us.

"If I've done anything in my life," said Jeff, "it would be pushing the spay/neuter agenda and training hundreds of veterinarians, over 1,500 at this point. I'm also really proud that we can help people and animals who are a part of our lives. And if we make a difference in the lives of people and animals, then I think we're doing something right."

The PPI Clinic in Conifer, Colorado

Epilogue

As a writer whose passion is to bring forth stories of inspirational people, it is my hope that this book about Dr. Jeff has done so.

From my first encounter with him, I was struck by both his presence and entelechy; his care and compassion for people, life, and animals. In writing his story, I discovered that Jeff has an uncanny ability, especially where animals are concerned, to set aside all the rhetoric of what "should" be done, and simply do what needs to be done by always asking, "What's in the animal's best interest?"

Did he make mistakes along the way or encounter obstacles? Of course! A life journey is not without mistakes and obstacles. However, no matter the setbacks, Jeff keeps going. He does not let anyone or anything deter him from his passion to help animals, not even multiple bouts with cancer.

Moreover, he consistently goes beyond the boundaries of normal physical endurance and what might be considered traditional animal care by providing low-cost veterinarian services affordable to all, by trying to save first rather than physically alter or euthanize, by working with *all* animals and, ultimately by paying it forward through training and educating other veterinarians.

He follows one simple passion and goal—to help as many animals as possible.

From the beginning, and even more so now as I conclude the writing of this book, I remain firm in my stance that Jeff's life is well worth documenting—an inspirational story of one veterinarian who dares to go beyond the boundaries and make a difference in the lives of people and animals all around the world. That's Dr. Jeff, the Rocky Mountain Vet.

~ Author's Collection ~

*Petra and Jeff at Harlan Street
clinic in Wheatridge,
March 2023*

*Jeff standing outside Conifer clinic
as remodeling is underway, March 2023*

*Conifer clinic remodeling, March 2023
Above: Jeff observing the progress
Right: Hector lends a hand*

*Celebrating the
Grand Opening of the
Conifer clinic
L to R: Melinda Grohol,
Petra, Jeff,
Melody Richardson
(Jeff's cousin),
Mike Richardson,
and Esther Mechler,
May 2023*

~ **Author's Collection** ~

Jeff on the homestead porch, May 2023

Jeff & Fred, October 2023

L to R: Tony, Mike Richardson, Jeff, and Melinda, at Jeff and Petra's Conifer home, 2023

The "cool" weather vane at Jeff and Petra's home

Fred, May 2019

~ Then & Now ~

*Street interview with local media
Fort Collins, Colorado*

*"Speak Out" event
Early activist work*

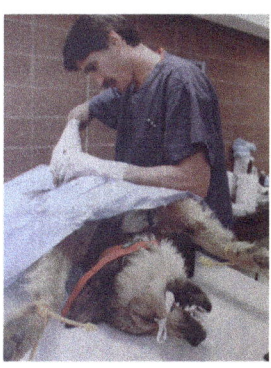

Jeff in action at the Crow Reservation clinic, early 1990s

Prep time at Mexican spay/neuter clinic site

Jeff on vacation in Greenland, 2024

Conifer Chamber of Commerce Awards Ceremony where Jeff served as presenter of the Non-Profit of the Year Award, April 2025

~ Native American Reservation Work ~

*Working with
Jean Atthowe's
Group
in Montana
1996*

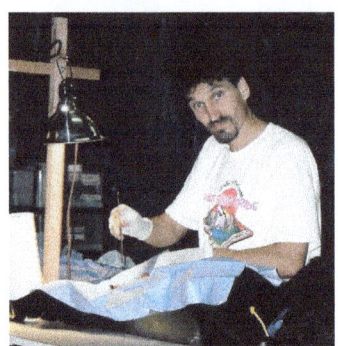

*Spay/neuter work at the
Fort Belknap Reservation*

Crow Reservation in Montana, 2001

*Tribute banner to
Jean Atthowe
on permanent
display at the
Planned Pethood
clinic in
Conifer,
Colorado*

*Jeff and his
volunteer group
enjoy some time at
Yellowstone National Park
after providing
free spay/neuter clinics
at multiple Native
American reservations,
August 2024*

~ Teaching and International Experiences ~

Adopt a Mongrel poster
India, 2000

Jeff and Esther Mechler at the
Asia for Animals Symposium
in Hong Kong, 2004

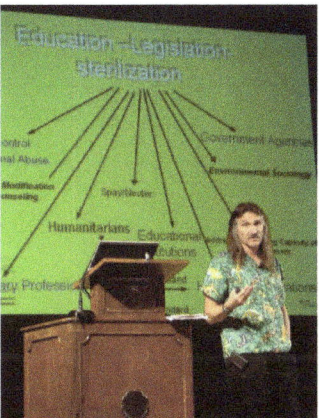

Lecture event
featuring the
Street Dog
Program, *2011*

Speaking at the
14th Annual International
Companion Animal
Welfare Conference in
Istanbul, Turkey,
October 2014

149

~ Teaching and International Experiences ~

The India Group, 2000

*House
dogs
in an
Indian
home*

*While in
India, Jeff
and
his group
"wash away
their sins"
by wading
in the
Ganges River*

~ Teaching and International Experiences ~

European Spay/Neuter Teaching and Lecture Trip to Croatia and Romania, October 2014

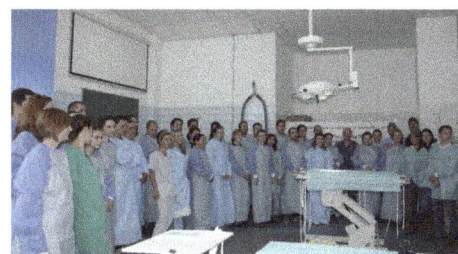

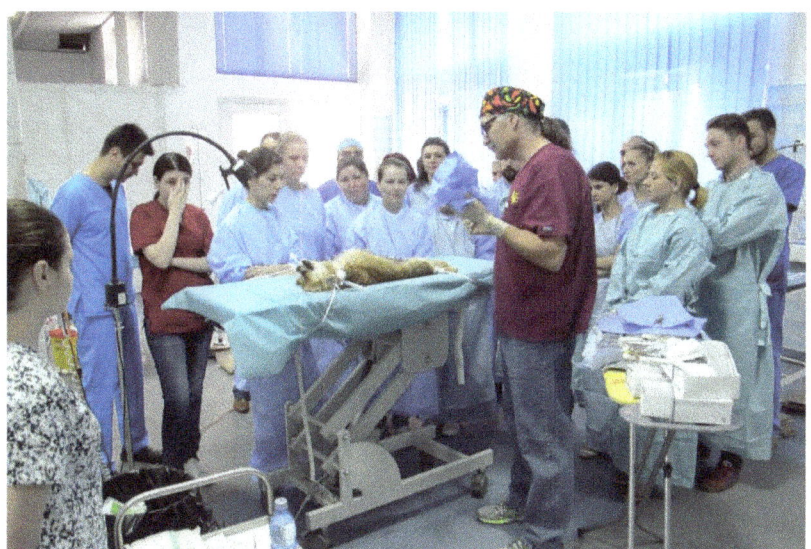

A teaching moment for veterinarians in training, country of Georgia located in the Caucasus mountain region on the coast of the Black Sea at the intersection of Eastern Europe and West Asia

~ Teaching and International Experiences ~

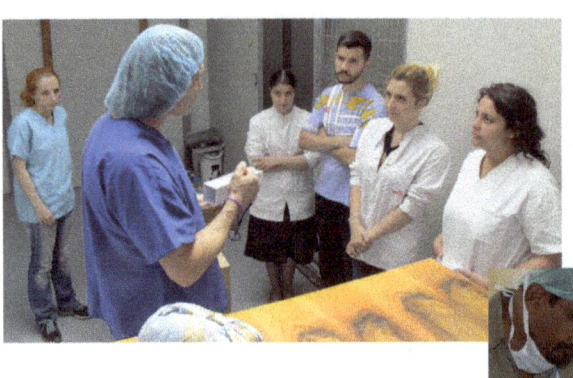

*Teaching
moments
in
Romania*

*Teaching
moments
in
India*

~ *Dr. Jeff Rocky Mountain Vet* ~

The Dr. Jeff Rocky Mountain Vet
*Film crew, Season 8
L to R, front row: Joshua White
and Levi Gilbert
L to R, back row: Chas Gordon,
James Tobin, Callie (Zanandrie)
Bochenek, Seth Blair, Steve LuKanic,
Heidi Gemer, Chas Isenhart*

Some of the cast on the
Dr. Jeff Rocky Mountain Vet *show
L to R, front row: Jeff, Petra, Hector
L to R, back row: Dr. Baier and Susan*

~ *Dr. Jeff Rocky Mountain Vet* ~

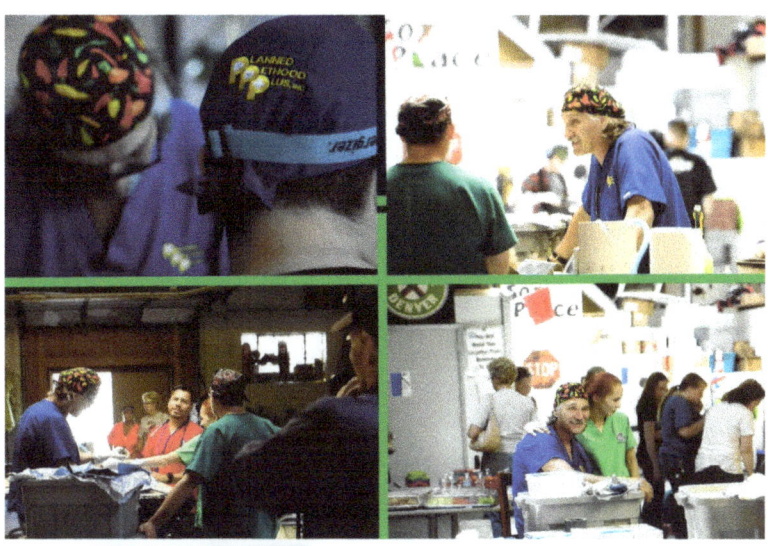

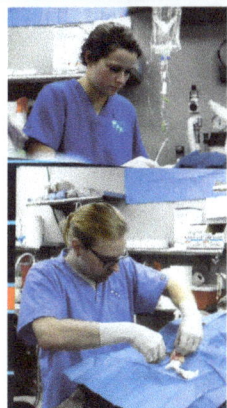

*Photo montage, from
Dr. Jeff's scrapbook*

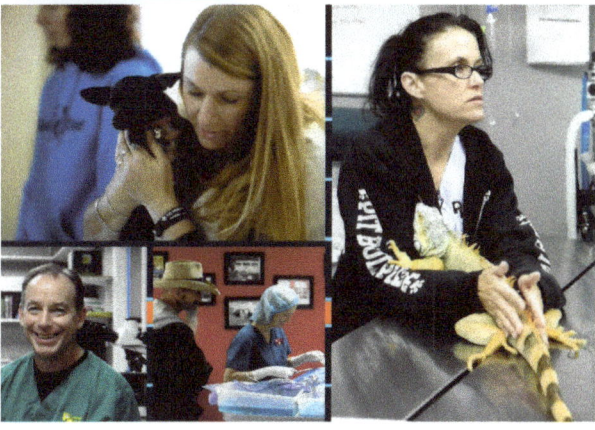

Melinda Grohol

~ *Dr. Jeff Rocky Mountain Vet* ~

Working with alligators at Colorado Gators Reptile Park

Lola the jaguar, post-surgery, just before being placed in the recovery pen

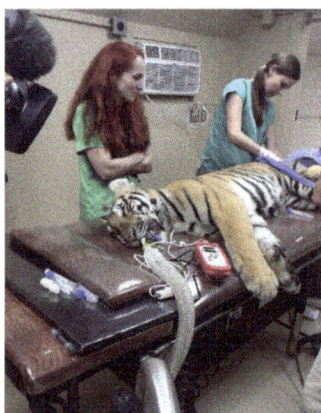

Petra watching a tiger being prepped for surgery

~ *Dr. Jeff Rocky Mountain Vet* ~

A promotional poster for the Dr. Jeff Rocky Mountain Vet *show*

~ North High School Running Team & Coaching Experience ~

The original invitation to join the
North High School Cross Country Running Team

Jeff and his runners, July 1997

~ North High School Running Team
& Coaching Experience ~

Team runner Joseph Manilafasha on the cover of Colorado Runner *magazine, January/February 2009 Issue*

Jeff and the 2006-2007 running team

Jeff and Hector celebrate after Hector runs a 100-mile marathon race in Leadville, Colorado

Jeff and his runners, 2011

157

THE PLANNED PETHOOD
INTERNATIONAL FOUNDATION
Making a world of difference in companion animal welfare

The Planned Pethood International Foundation, a 501(c)(3) organization, encompasses two entities: Planned Pethood International, PPI, and the Intermountain Humane Society, IMH.

Our Mission: The reduction of companion animal overpopulation throughout the world.

Core Values: We believe that neither euthanasia nor the use of limited resources to warehouse a large number of animals is the solution to companion animal overpopulation. Only through the reduction in population via spay/neuter and affordable veterinary care available to all will the status of companion animals be elevated and ensure their safety and well-being.

Our Methodology: Our efforts include spay/neuter campaigns; training veterinarians to continue the work of spay/neuter and affordable care; and developing culturally relevant educational materials to help influence future societal concepts, beliefs, and actions about companion animal welfare.

To that end, Planned Pethood International through Dr. Jeff Young, DVM, continually makes presentations and conducts sterilization campaigns at locations in the United States, on numerous Native American reservations, and locales globally including Slovakia, India, Panama, Hungary, Mexico, Poland, and Turkey. Currently, Planned Pethood International is active in veterinary hospitals located in Bratislava, Slovakia, and Merida (Mexico).

Further, Planned Pethood International continues to provide training services for veterinarians from around the world at either of its two training centers located in Conifer, Colorado and Puerto Morelos, Mexico.

158

Veterinarians in the Planned Pethood International training programs are never charged and are also provided with free room and board during their training.

Planned Pethood International Goals
- To reduce companion animal overpopulation throughout the world while elevating the status of our companion animal friends.
- Continue to work placing emphasis on resolving the problem of companion animal overpopulation through education, legislation, and spay/neuter programs, NOT BY WAREHOUSING OR EUTHANIZING ANIMALS.
- Continue to invest the money from our active adoption program and donations to provide training and equipment for veterinarians who want the opportunity to advance the condition of companion animals around the world.
- Continue to support our established veterinary hospitals in Bratislava, Slovakia, Merida, and our newest international training center in Puerto Morelos in the state of Yucatán Mexico.
- Build a state-of-the-art hospital in Asia emphasizing spay/neuter while working closely with local veterinarians and animal welfare groups.

No one group is committed to these goals more than Planned Pethood International, and with your tax-deductible donation, you too can be a part of companion animal history and welfare. 100% of all contributions and fundraising money go directly to reducing companion animal overpopulation, training veterinarians in safe and efficient spay/neuter techniques, or helping abused and abandoned animals.

To learn more or to donate, please visit our website at
https://www.plannedpethoodinternational.org
or call us at (303) 433-3291

Our address: Planned Pethood International,
11825 U.S. HWY 285, Conifer, CO 80433

Spay/Neuter Basics

S paying and neutering are the single most important and effective methods for preventing unplanned or unwanted litters and reducing animal overpopulation whether for domestic pets, or roaming and feral animal groups.

Although progress has been made in recent years, millions of unwanted dogs and cats are still euthanized each year, including puppies and kittens. The good news is that you can make a difference. By having your pet spayed or neutered you will help to prevent the birth of unwanted animals.

Spaying/neutering your pets is also highly cost-effective. The cost of your pet's spay/neuter surgery is far less than the cost of having and caring for a litter of animals, trying to find good homes for all the animals in a litter, or sending the animals out to fend for themselves and adding to the feral population.

What is spay/neuter?

Spaying involves removing the uterus and ovaries of a female animal, and neutering removes the testicles of a male animal. These procedures make sure that your animal will not be able to reproduce.

The Benefits of Spay/Neuter
- Reduces spraying and marking behaviors
- Reduces roaming
- Reduces aggression
- Lowers risks of cancers
- Decreases pet overpopulation
- Increases life span up to 3-5 years

When to Spay/Neuter

For dogs: The recommended time to spay or neuter a dog is six to nine months. All things considered, if your dog is healthy, there is no specific age limit to having the procedure done.

160

Note: When it comes to dogs, there is no one-size-fits-all recommendation for the optimal timing of spaying or neutering. Consulting with your local veterinarian can help you decide on the best timing to spay/neuter your dog based on its breed, temperament, environment, and overall health.

For cats: It is generally considered safe for kittens as young as eight weeks old to be spayed or neutered. To help avoid the start of urine spraying and eliminate the chance for pregnancy, it is recommended to spay/neuter your cat before they reach five months of age.

Note: The AVMA, American Association of Feline Practitioners, Association of Shelter Veterinarians, and several cat advocacy groups support spaying or neutering of cats by five months of age. This recommendation is based on the known benefits of sterilization, and the lack of evidence of harm related to the age when the procedure is performed.

*Contrary to popular belief,
there is no known benefit to delaying the spay procedure
until a female dog or cat has gone through their first heat cycle.

Where can I find low-cost spay/neuter services for my pet?

United Spay Alliance is a non-profit organization dedicated to promoting affordable, accessible, and timely spay/neuter services across the United States. Among its numerous services and educational outreach programs is a nationwide Spay/Neuter Referral Directory.

To locate a low-cost, spay/neuter provider near you, go to the United Spay Alliance homepage at **www.unitedspayalliance.org**, and click on the FIND LOW-COST SPAY/NEUTER PROVIDERS link located at the top of the page. Then, follow the prompts providing your state, zip code, and search radius to receive a list of veterinarians in your area performing low-cost spay/neuter services.

A Final Note About Spay/Neuter

If you are concerned about pet and animal overpopulation, overcrowded shelters, and the euthanasia of animals in general, here are some other things you can do to help.

- Adopt a pet from a shelter that performs spay/neuter before adopting out
- Support or donate to animal welfare organizations that promote and uphold spay/neuter as part of their mission
- Support Trap-Neuter-Release (TNR) programs that help control feral animal populations
- Volunteer at your local shelter, veterinarian's office, or with other animal rescue programs in your area

THE VETERINARY OATH

Being admitted to the profession
of veterinary medicine,
I solemnly swear to use my
scientific knowledge and skills
for the benefit of society
through the protection of
animal health and welfare,
the prevention and relief of
animal suffering,
the conservation of animal resources,
the promotion of public health,
and the
advancement of medical knowledge.

I will practice my profession conscientiously,
with dignity, and in keeping with
the principles of veterinary medical ethics.

I accept as a lifelong obligation
the continual improvement
of my professional knowledge
and competence.

Melinda Grohol

ACCREDITED VETERINARY COLLEGES - UNITED STATES

State	College Name
Alabama	Auburn University
	Tuskegee University
Arizona	University of Arizona
	Midwestern University
California	Western University of Health Sciences
	University of California
Colorado	Colorado State University
Florida	University of Florida
Georgia	University of Georgia
Illinois	University of Illinois
Indiana	Purdue University
Iowa	Iowa State University
Kansas	Kansas State University
Louisiana	Louisiana State University
Massachusetts	Tufts University
Michigan	Michigan State University
Minnesota	University of Minnesota
Mississippi	Mississippi State University
Missouri	University of Missouri
New York	Cornell University
	Long Island University
North Carolina	North Carolina State University
Ohio	Ohio State University
Oklahoma	Oklahoma State University
Oregon	Oregon State University
Pennsylvania	University of Pennsylvania
Tennessee	Lincoln Memorial University
	University of Tennessee
Texas	Texas A&M University
	Texas Tech University

164

Virginia .... Virginia Tech University
Washington .... Washington State University
Wisconsin .... University of Wisconsin

ACCREDITED VETERINARY COLLEGES - CANADA

Province	College Name
Alberta	University of Calgary
Ontario	University of Guelph
Prince Edward Island	University of Prince Edward Island
Quebec	Université de Montréal
Saskatchewan	University of Saskatchewan

ACCREDITED VETERINARY COLLEGES – INTERNATIONAL

Country	College Name
Australia	Murdoch University
	The University of Sydney
	University of Melbourne
	University of Queensland
France	Vetagro Sup
Ireland	University College, Dublin
Korea	Seoul National University
Mexico	Universidad Nacional Autónoma de México
Netherlands	State University of Utrecht
New Zealand	Massey University College of Sciences
Scotland	University of Glasgow
	University of Edinburgh
United Kingdom	The Royal Veterinary College
	University of Bristol
	University of Nottingham
	University of Liverpool
West Indies	Ross University
	St. George's University

EPISODE LISTING FOR THE *DR. JEFF ROCKY MOUNTAIN VET* SHOW AIRED ON THE ANIMAL PLANET NETWORK

Season (S) / Episode (E)

SEASON 1

S1, E 1: One More Chance

S1, E 2: Whatever IT Takes

S1, E 3: Dr. Jeff: Rocky Mountain Vet

S1, E 4: Rocks and Crocs

S1, E 5: Mile High Mutt

S1, E 6: Street Dog

S1, E 7: A Full Heart

S1, E 8: Feline Face Lift

S1, E 9: Miracle Cat

S1, E10: Holiday Miracles

SEASON 2

S2, E 1: Nine Lives

S2, E 2: Temperature's Rising

S2, E 3: Saved by the Sky

S2, E 4: Beware of Cat

S2, E 5: The Lion's Den

S2, E 6: Mission Beyond

S2, E 7: Tender Loving Care

S2, E 8: Risky Business

S2, E 9: A Second Chance

S2, E10: Sioux Journey

S2, E11: Turning Point

S2, E12: New World

SEASON 3

S3, E 1: Full Speed Ahead

S3, E 2: Race Against Time

S3, E 3: A Long Way From Home

S3, E 4: On the Edge

S3, E 5: Born to Run

S3, E 6: Friends for Life

S3, E 7: Shelter from the Storm

S3, E 8: Picking Up the Pieces

S3, E 9: Never Give Up

S3, E10: Unlucky Break

S3, E11: A Fighting Chance

S3, E12: Last Hope

SEASON 4

S4, E 1: A Little Miracle

S4, E 2: Lily's Puppy Mill Rescue

S4, E 3: Hog Wild

S4, E 4: The Dog Who Won Jeff's Heart

S4, E 5: Into the Jungle

S4, E 6: Saving Bear

S4, E 7: The Heart of a Pit Bull

S4, E 8: The Littlest Patients

S4, E 9: A Far Away Home

S4, E10: He's Ours Now

SEASON 5

S5, E 1: Close to Home

S5, E 2: A Tiny Miracle

S5, E 3: A Brave Pit Bull

S5, E 4: Lion Country

S5, E 5: A Horse of a Different Color

S5, E 6: A Fighting Spirit

S5, E 7: The Road Home

S5, E 8: Pit Bull vs. Rattler

S5, E 9: Care for Bear

S5, E10: Safe from the Storm

S5, E11: Nalla Fights Back

S5, E12: Help on the Street

SEASON 6

S6, E 1: At Home With Wolves

S6, E 2: A Brave Little Dog

S6, E 3: Blown Away

S6, E 4: A Lucky Break

S6, E 5: Runaway Dog

S6, E 6: A Tiger's Tale

S6, E 7: Tiny Soul Mate

S6, E 8: Happy Couple of Camels

S6, E 9: Head Over Heels

S6, E10: Ready to Roll

S6, E11: The Cutest Yak in Colorado

S6, E12: A Wild Ride

S6, E13: Family Reunion

S6, E14: Dr. Jeff: Pandemic Emergency

SEASON 7

S7, E 1: A First for Dr. Jeff

S7, E 2: Miracle on the Freeway

S7, E 3: Fainting Goat Ranch

S7, E 4: Mission in South Dakota

S7, E 5: Petra's Pigs

S7, E 6: Jeff and the Jaguar

S7, E 7: Bison Wranglers

S7, E 8: Frenchie With a Bump

S7, E 9: Gator Tale

S7, E10: Naked Kitten's New Dad

S7, E11: The Littlest Rescue

S7, E12: Kino's Mystery

S7, E13: Dr. Jeff: 30-Year Ride

SEASON 8

S8, E 1: A New Adventure

S8, E 2: Rise to the Challenge

S8, E 3: Little Puppy, Big Heart

S8, E 4: Making A Splash

S8, E 5: Hero Dog

S8, E 6: Wild at Heart

S8, E 7: New Body for Lolly

S8, E 8: Old Dog, New Hope

S8, E 9: Healing Farm

S8, E10: Adoption Stories

ACKNOWLEDGEMENTS

A heartfelt thank you to my daughter Ginny Grohol,
Esther Mechler, and Steve LuKanic for believing in me, this book,
and being my support team as well as my editing team.

Jeff, Esther, and Steve, from the first moment I met each of you,
I felt as if we had been friends for years.
There was an instant connection and I am grateful
for our continuing friendship.
Thank you for trusting and working with me.

Thank you to all of Jeff's colleagues, staff, family, and friends
who shared their insights, photos, and personal stories.

Thank you to all my friends, family, and co-workers
who listened to me talk about this book and my plans,
sometimes incessantly... especially Mikey
who literally gave me a *"That's awesome!"* high-five
each and every time I talked about the book with him,
even if it was revision #42, only a slight twist in the process,
or a moment of new-found inspiration.

Thank you to my brother Christopher,
who mowed my lawn for me
during those summer and fall seasons
so I could devote my time to writing this book.

Thank you to God and my angel helpers,
humans and animals alike,
for enabling me to manifest, design, and publish this book.

ABOUT THE AUTHOR
MELINDA GROHOL

A longtime freelance writer, Melinda is passionate about sharing the
stories of people who make a difference in life.
Beyond writing, her career path also includes marketing,
advertising, graphic design, promotions, stage acting,
and more than a decade of bookselling experience.

A voracious reader of all genres with a penchant for children's books,
cozy mysteries, and Scooby Doo, Melinda loves books that have
characters who inspire readers to take action and
add positivity into the world.
She resides in Mentor, Ohio with her two tuxedo cats,
Sophie and Tillie.

L to R:
Daughter Ginny
and Melinda

L to R:
Tillie and
Sophie

www.ingramcontent.com/pod-product-compliance
Lightning Source LLC
Chambersburg PA
CBHW051520120626
46551CB00012B/1007